The World's 100 Best Recipes

The World's 100 Best Recipes

by Roland Gööck

Culinary Arts Institute

1727 South Indiana Avenue, Chicago, Illinois 60616

Introduction

The idea of choosing the world's one hundred best recipes, photographing them in a beautiful setting and adapting them for preparation in home kitchens throughout the world was that of a distinguished German writer on food, Roland Gööck. His book, published as *Die 100 berühmtesten Rezepte der Welt,* has sold more than 100,000 copies in the German-speaking world.

Herr Gööck made no claim to his compilation being a definitive or an all-inclusive cookbook. His choices, he pointed out, were based on meals he had eaten in cities all over the world, and, because tastes differ, he notes that other people might have made other choices. But his objective was to give the readers of this book some new ideas for meals and to inspire them to look at food in a new way.

If you, like Herr Gööck, find the subject of food absorbing, you are in good company. Some of the world's greatest philosophers, writers, and artists have shared your interest. Immanuel Kant, for example, was concerned with every detail of his household's menus. The famous philosopher would discuss food instead of his categorical imperative with admiring lady visitors. Other great figures such as Blaise Pascal, Arthur Schopenhauer Gioacchino Rossini, Alexandre Dumas, Honoré de Balzac and Johann Wolfgang von Goethe were all known for their love of food.

The unashamed hedonism of both gourmet and gourmand has brought criticism, of course. René Descartes, another philosopher, had a witty answer to such a critic. "Do you believe, then," he asked, "that nature produces all these good things for dullards only?"

Because food is basic not only to the sustenance but also the quality of life, a history of food is in many ways the story of the human race. Who knows, really, how much food has affected the course of history?

From the beginning of civilization, great men have been influenced by the diplomacy of the dining table. Cleopatra enticed Antony with dozens of aphrodisiac delights, served on golden dishes set with precious stones. In the Middle Ages, great feasts and banquets celebrated royal marriages, the signing of treaties, and victories in battle.

By the sixteenth century, European rulers were competing over the lavishness of their tables. The French food encyclopedia, *Larousse Gastronomique,* describes a banquet given by the city of Paris in 1549 to welcome Catherine de Medici. The menu included, in addition to enormous numbers of vegetable dishes and ordinary meat dishes, "30 peacocks, 33 pheasants, 21 swans, 9 cranes, 33 ducks, 33 ibises, 33 egrets, 33 young herons, 30 young goats, 99 young pigeons, 99 turtle doves, 13 partridges, 33 goslings, 3 young bustards, 13 young capons, 90 quails, 66 boiling chickens, 66 Indian chickens, 30 capons, 90 spring chickens in vinegar, and 66 chickens cooked as grouse."

Menus at state banquets in the seventeenth and eighteenth centuries were even more incredible. There were usually seven or eight courses, with dozens of dishes in each course. The Bourbon kings of France, especially Louis XIV and Louis XV, were noted for their sumptuous dining. They encouraged their nobles to keep extravagant tables, and court protocol at Versailles revolved around meals. Talleyrand, the powerful French diplomat and statesman, depended on his dinners for a large part of his diplomatic success. His cook, Carême, is considered one of the greatest chefs in history. When Talleyrand went to Louis XVIII to get his final briefing for the Congress of Vienna, he told the king, "Sire, I have more need of casseroles than of written instructions."

The pattern set by the rulers and diplomats of the past prevails today. Visiting dignitaries are welcomed at formal banquets, and menus are carefully chosen to make the right impression. Future food historians will probably include the menu served to United States President Richard M. Nixon, on his recent visit to China, among the historically important banquets.

It is not only the gastronomic tastes of the rulers and diplomats that have affected history, but also the demands of the average citizen. For centuries, the spice trade dominated the European and Middle Eastern economy; public demand for spices eventually led to the discovery of the New World. Sugar, of which the Elizabethans were so fond, commanded high prices, and the competition for the sugar trade between European countries became fierce. When the Europeans discovered coffee, trade with Turkey and Java increased. Chocolate, tea, oranges and pineapples all have similar histories; when these foods became the fashion, trading systems were developed to meet the demand.

Just as food has influenced world development, so have trade and military expansion influenced eating habits. In the early centuries of civilization, Egyptian and Phoenician traders brought the olive tree and the grape vine to all the shores of the Mediterranean; today, the Mediterranean countries retain their dependence on these foods. Turkish conquests of the Balkan countries, North Africa, and Spain added an oriental touch to the cooking in these areas. The discovery of the Western Hemisphere changed the European diet.

Trade in food has been so extensive that there is probably no dish that is not really international in origin. The common potato, a basic ingredient of many diverse dishes, was not even introduced into Europe until the sixteenth century. The tomato, the basis of today's Italian food, was also a Latin-American import. Lemons were brought to Europe from India. Melons came from Asia to Italy, where they were considered delicacies by the Greeks and Romans. And, of course, everyone knows that the American Indians taught the first European settlers how to grow maize, or corn. But in spite of the international sources of many ingredients, the world's countries have developed an amazing variety of dishes, and it is with that variety that this book deals. The rice for paella may have come from India or Egypt, the saffron may have originated in Asia, but paella itself is Spanish.

Today, more than ever before, cooking is becoming international. The ordinary cook now has access to a greater variety of foods than were served at the most luxurious tables of the past.

The development of passenger airplanes and the decrease in the cost of transportation have resulted in more people having time and enough money to travel all over the world and adventurous tourists have grown fond of new dishes they have encountered in strange countries. And, since the nineteenth century, a great tide of immigration has brought new ethnic groups to many formerly homogeneous countries, where they have established restaurants and enabled the people among whom they live to become knowledgeable about their cuisine. Chinese restaurants, for example, exist all over the United States; Indonesian restaurants are popular in the home of *haute cuisine,* Paris; Hungarian eating places can be found in Australia, South Africa, and Canada; and London restaurants offer specialties from every exotic corner of the world, including their former colonies in America.

These one hundred recipes reflect the new international approach to good cooking and better eating. They have been chosen for their quality and their long-lasting popularity. They are not necessarily dishes which can be described as *haute cuisine.* Many of them are hearty provincial specialties, whose naturally fine flavors are enhanced by the special approach to cooking characteristic of the country of origin.

The recipes for these dishes have been adapted for use in kitchens in English-speaking countries throughout the world by the coordinated efforts of the staff of the Culinary Arts Institute in the United States and the food editors of cooperating publishers in England and Australia, so that regional and national differences have been taken into full consideration.

But, as the old saying goes, the proof of the pudding is in the eating. *Bon appetit!*

Contents

Angels on Horseback
England

Angels on Horseback are a specialty of English cuisine but are also known in other countries; in France, for example, they are called Anges à Cheval. They are usually served as appetizers and consist of raw oysters wrapped in thin slices of bacon and broiled until the bacon is browned and crisp. Thinly sliced smoked ham may be substituted for bacon, if desired.

In many areas, oysters are gathered only during the months that contain an ''r'' in their names (September through April). During the other months they may be purchased frozen or canned; but many gourmets do not consider such oysters to be as desirable as the fresh oysters. Nowadays, only a fraction of the oysters are gathered from natural oyster beds. Most of them come from ''oyster parks'' which are seawater-filled brick basins near a coast.

12 to 16 medium oysters. Freshly ground pepper
12 to 16 thin slices bacon. 1 lemon, thinly sliced

Open oysters. (Use only tightly closed oysters; discard the half-opened ones.) Season oysters with pepper and wrap a slice of bacon around each; secure with a wooden pick or skewer. Arrange in shallow baking pan and place in a hot oven (425°F or 220°C) just until bacon is crisp. (It is a good idea to pre-cook the bacon slightly to shorten the baking time, as oysters must *never be overcooked.* Bacon should still be limp after pre-cooking so it can be easily rolled around oysters.) Garnish plate with lemon slices and *parsley.* Serve hot on *toast.*

If desired, oysters may be broiled, placing them about 4 inches (10 centimeters) from the broiler heat. Broil 7 to 8 minutes, turning several times to brown bacon evenly.
About 4 servings.

Bern Councillors' Plate
Switzerland

In addition to being the seat of the Swiss Federal Government, Bern is famous for its nutritious meat plates. There is, for example, a plate consisting of sausage, bacon, ham, and salted meat on a bed of sauerkraut. However, the Ratsherrenplatte (city councillors' plate), described below, is more elaborate. It combines the so-called Rosti (Swiss-style fried potatoes) with various small fillets and other quickly cooked delicacies. This particular dish is intended to be served as a snack for the city councillors after their meeting, but can just as well be served for lunch.

The dish may be prepared in a simplified manner by offering only one kind of fillet (beef or veal) with the pork sausages.

5 medium potatoes. Salt
4 tablespoons shortening
2 medium onions, chopped and fried
8 thin slices lean bacon, crisply fried
4 slices veal liver or veal kidneys
4 small beef fillets. 4 veal fillets
4 small pork sausages

Pare and thinly slice the potatoes. Season to taste and fry in shortening until golden, turning occasionally. Just before potatoes are done, distribute them evenly in the skillet and finish frying just as you would an omelet. Keeping "potato cake" intact, transfer to a pre-heated plate. Top with the golden-fried onions and crisp bacon.

Meanwhile, fry liver (or kidneys), beef and veal fillets, and pork sausages separately and serve with the potatoes. If desired, use other meat such as pork fillets, sweetbreads, or brains. Garnish plate with *tomato wedges* and *parsley*.
4 servings

Bigos
Poland

The method of preparing this Polish national dish, also spelled Bigosch or Bigusch (or hunters' stew), varies throughout Poland. According to culinary history, the stew was prepared with cabbage, onions, mushrooms, and a variety of other vegetables along with apples and prunes. Game was the main ingredient, often leftover game.

Bigos as it is served today is quite different from the early versions, but the character of the dish is somewhat the same. For instance, pork is sometimes substituted for game and in some regions even chicken is used.

Bigos can be served as a casserole or as an appetizer in which case it is eaten right out of the dish in which it was prepared. An eighteenth century eating rule goes as follows: after having uncovered the casserole, remove pieces of meat with a fork, letting them drip on a piece of bread held in your left hand, and eat; then follow with the bread. Here is a recipe for Bigos made with cabbage:

¼ lb. (125 g.) lean smoked bacon
1 lb. (500 g.) pork. 3 onions, coarsely chopped
¼ lb. (125 g.) garlic sausage, sliced
1¾ lbs. (875 g.) cabbage, coarsely shredded
¼ lb. (125 g.) mushrooms, sliced
1 small can tomato purée. 2 cloves garlic, crushed
1 teaspoon cumin seed. 2 teaspoons paprika
Marjoram. Salt. 1 bay leaf
2 cups (½ liter or about 1 pt.) white wine

Dice bacon and pork; brown well in large skillet along with the onion. Add sliced sausage, shredded cabbage, mushrooms, tomato purée, crushed garlic, and seasonings. Turn mixture into a large casserole; add white wine, and just enough *water* to cover all ingredients. Cover casserole tightly; cook without stirring in a moderate oven (350° F or 180° C), about 1½ hours, or until done. Serve hot or lukewarm with dark bread.
About 6 servings

Pears Hélène
France

This dessert of classic French cuisine is called Poires Belle Hélène. The dessert is named for the beautiful Helen who, according to Greek legend, caused the Trojan War. However, in Helen's time, ice cream was probably unheard of, and chocolate was only known in the Old World long after Troy had been buried under ashes and rubble. On the other hand, it is quite possible that Trojans did know a kind of pear.

It can truly be said, however, that this refreshing dessert does pay homage to one of the most beautiful women of legend. From the culinary standpoint, the dessert is as easy and simple to prepare as it is attractive to behold. The only problem one might encounter is in the pouring of the hot sauce over a chilled dessert, which can cause the ice cream to melt too rapidly. This can be avoided by simply serving the chocolate sauce in a separate dish. The truly classic French recipe does not call for whipped cream as does the recipe below. Instead, each serving is decorated with crystallized violets. Here is our recipe:

8 poached pear halves (see below)
1 pt. (250 g.) firm vanilla ice cream
Chocolate sauce or chocolate syrup, heated
Whipped cream, sweetened with vanilla-flavoured sugar

Spoon some of the ice cream in bottom of four individual dishes. Arrange poached pear halves, rounded side up, over ice cream. Top pears with remaining ice cream. Drizzle hot chocolate sauce over ice cream and pears, or serve the sauce separately. Garnish with sweetened whipped cream. Accompany with rolled wafers.
4 servings

To poach pears: Remove skins from pears; halve pears and remove cores. Prepare a syrup as follows: combine *2 cups (400 grams or 14 ounces) granulated sugar* with *1 cup (¼ liter or about ½ pint)* water in a saucepan. Cook rapidly 5 minutes and add *1 teaspoon vanilla extract.* Add *pears* and cook gently until almost tender (not soft), 5 to 8 minutes. Lift pears from syrup, drain well and chill thoroughly before serving. If desired, drained canned pears may be substituted for the poached pears.

Beef Stroganoff
Soviet Union

This well known dish was reputedly named for the Stroganoffs, a dynasty of wealthy merchants from Novgorod who had reached the height of their power in the eighteenth century. By the sixteenth century the Stroganoffs owned land and salt refineries in the Urals, which at that time was the eastern border of Russian rule. They initiated the advance over the Urals that ended in Siberia's submission. Today, the imperial life they led sounds like something from a fairy tale.

2 onions, coarsely chopped
3 tablespoons butter. 4 tablespoons flour
1 cup (¼ liter or about ½ pt.) beef broth or bouillon
Dry mustard. Salt. Lemon juice
½ to 1 cup (115 to 230 g. or ¼ to ½ pt.) thick sour cream
4 oz. (125 g.) mushrooms, sliced and lightly
browned in butter
2 gherkins, finely sliced
1 lb. (500 g.) beef sirloin or tenderloin
3 tablespoons butter

Cook chopped onion in butter in a heavy saucepan until golden. Stir in the flour, then the broth; cook and stir until mixture comes to boiling; cook 5 minutes longer. Stir in the mustard, salt, and lemon juice. Blend in sour cream. Add the sliced mushrooms and gherkins and bring just to boiling. Cut meat into serving-sized pieces or long narrow strips and quickly brown in remaining butter in a skillet. (Do not over-cook; meat should be pink inside.) Combine the sauce with browned meat and heat to serving temperature (do not boil). If desired, tomato wedges may be added to the sauce. Serve Stroganoff with fried potatoes, cooked noodles, rice, or bread dumplings.
About 4 servings

Bollito Misto
Italy

The name for this specialty from northern Italy literally means "cooked mixture." It consists mainly of several kinds of meat, also chicken, cooked whole or in large pieces then cut into serving-sized portions at the table. The combination of meats used in this version of the dish can be varied somewhat, but it should include beef, veal, tongue, and chicken. It may be complemented with garlic sausages and pork. A variety of hot and cold sauces and salads may also be served with it. However, the cold herb sauce (Salsa Verde) is a must.

This recipe for Bollito Misto is a generous one suitable for a company dinner.

1 beef tongue. 1 calf's head
2 lbs. (1 kg.) beef (loin or neck)
1 stewing chicken. 2 pig's feet
Soup greens (see note). Salt
3 hard-cooked eggs
½ cup (⅛ liter or about ¼ pt.) salad oil
3 tablespoons wine vinegar
Sugar. Salt, pepper
6 tablespoons chopped herbs

Combine meats, chicken and soup greens in a steam pressure cooker. Add salt to taste and cook according to manufacturer's cooking timetable. Remove skin from tongue. Arrange hot meats on a large board. Serve with boiled potatoes, cooked carrots, cabbage, celery salad, beet salad, small gherkins, mixed pickles and Salsa Verde.
Salsa Verde: Finely chop eggs. Combine oil and wine vinegar. Add sugar, salt and pepper to taste. Mix well and combine with chopped eggs and a blend of herbs such as dill, tarragon, chervil, parsley, sorrel and chives. Refrigerate sauce several hours to allow flavors to blend.
10 to 12 servings
Note: For soup greens, use all or a choice of the following vegetables (carrot, celery, leek, onion, parsnip, turnip) and herbs (parsley, tarragon, thyme).

Borscht
Soviet Union

This hearty soup originating in Russia has many variations. Generally speaking, Borscht refers to a beet soup made with or without meat, served hot or cold. However, many versions, like the one below, call for cabbage, tomatoes, and other colorful vegetables along with the beets. "If you have a good wife and a fat rich Borscht, be content!" says an old Russian proverb. So try this recipe and accompany with hearty buckwheat groats (Kasha).

1 lb. (500 g.) beef, cubed. 1½ teaspoons salt
¼ to ½ teaspoon pepper. 2 garlic cloves, crushed
1 large onion, coarsely chopped. 2 large carrots, diced
2 potatoes, pared and cubed. Butter or margarine
½ medium head cabbage, coarsely shredded
4 tomatoes, peeled and cut in pieces
1 can sliced beets with liquid
2 tablespoons vinegar. Snipped parsley
1 cup (230 g. or about ½ pt.) thick sour cream
8 oz. (250 g.) buckwheat groats (for Kasha)

Combine beef, salt, pepper, garlic and about *6 cups (1½ liter or about 1½ quarts) boiling water* in a large saucepot. Cover; bring to boiling; lower heat and simmer until meat is almost tender.

Meanwhile, lightly brown onion, carrot and potato in several tablespoons butter; add to saucepot and bring to boiling; add cabbage. Cook until meat and vegetables are tender; add tomatoes, beets (with cooking liquid) and vinegar; season soup to taste and heat thoroughly. Garnish with parsley and serve with sour cream.

To make Kasha: Brown the buckwheat groats in *2 or 3 tablespoons (30 or 40 grams or 1 or 1½ ounces) butter* or *margarine* in ovenproof casserole or baking dish. Add enough *boiling salted water* to cover buckwheat; cover tightly and bake in a moderate oven (350°-375°F or 180°-190°C) until done. Add more water, if needed, during baking. To serve, make "wells" in top of hot Kasha and fill cavities with browned butter or margarine. Serve with the hot soup.
8 to 10 servings

Boston Baked Beans
United States, Canada

Baked beans, Boston style, originated in early colonial times and, though considered a New England specialty, are popular throughout the United States and Canada. Years ago lumbermen along the Canadian border would cook beans once a week, freeze them and cut off a chunk when needed, to be heated in an iron pot. Baked beans were especially liked by the Puritans of New England because they could be prepared on the Holy Sabbath without much work or supervision. The original recipe used maple syrup, which has always been available in New England. However, molasses and even brown sugar are often used instead. New Englanders bake their beans slowly, often for six to eight hours.

1 lb. (500 g.) dried navy (pea) beans
2 teaspoons salt. 2 medium onions
Whole cloves (about 1 teaspoon)
⅓ cup (75 g. or 2½ oz.) firmly packed brown sugar
3 to 4 tablespoons molasses or maple syrup
1 teaspoon dry mustard. ½ teaspoon black pepper
½ lb. (250 g.) salt pork, cut in slices

Sort and wash beans thoroughly. Soak overnight in salted water to cover.

The following day, cook the beans 30 minutes; drain. Insert cloves in onions; put into a bean pot (or casserole) having a tight-fitting cover. Pour half the beans over the onions. Combine most of the brown sugar, the molasses, mustard and pepper with *2 cups (½ liter) hot water* and pour over beans. Add the meat and cover with remaining beans.

Bake in a slow oven (300°F or 150°C), 3 to 4 hours. During the last 30 minutes, remove cover, sprinkle beans with remaining brown sugar and bake until done. Add hot water during baking, if needed. Serve with Boston brown bread.
About 8 servings

Bourride (Fish Soup)
France

This hearty soup is a favorite of Provence, a seaside province where the people enjoy everything produced in the region. That would include plenty of fish, of the firm, white varieties used for this soup, called Bourride in Provence. Haddock, halibut, sole, perch and parts of the cod are all used.

The soup is served in a large bowl over toasted French bread (croûte) with a piece of fish topped with the mayonnaise sauce.

2 lbs. (1 kg.) assorted fish and seafood
½ to ¾ cup (120 to 175 ml.) white wine
1 large onion, coarsely chopped
1 large leek (white part only), thinly sliced
1 garlic clove, crushed. 1 to 2 tablespoons white wine vinegar. 1 small bay leaf. ¼ teaspoon fennel seed
1 to 1½ teaspoons salt
Thyme, parsley. 3 egg yolks. Garlic powder
⅔ cup (125 g. or about ¼ pt.) mayonnaise
Toasted French bread

Clean fish and cut into serving-sized pieces. Cover heads, fins and bones with 4 cups *(about 1 liter) water;* bring to boiling. Add the wine, vegetables; vinegar and seasonings; lower heat and simmer about 30 minutes. Strain the court bouillon through a sieve into a saucepan, pressing some of the vegetables through sieve. Bring bouillon to boiling and add fish pieces. Cook, uncovered, over low heat 6 to 8 minutes, or only until fish flakes easily but is still firm. Remove pieces of fish to a heated platter and keep warm. Beat the egg yolks slightly and blend in about ½ cup (⅛ liter) hot bouillon. Return to remaining bouillon in saucepan. Cook and stir over low heat until slightly thickened. Do not boil. Season to taste with *salt, pepper* and, if desired, *lemon juice.*

Combine garlic powder with mayonnaise in a bowl.

To serve, place toast slices in soup plates and ladle soup over slices. Serve fish and mayonnaise separately.

4 servings

9

Poularde de Bruxelles
Belgium

Poularde with tender Brussels sprouts (choux de Bruxelles) is a traditional Belgium holiday specialty. The plump chickens that are used may be fried, stewed or stuffed and roasted. Any stuffing may be prepared, but for special occasions, gourmets usually prefer a stuffing of chestnuts, chicken liver and truffles.

1 medium roasting chicken (3½ to 5½ lbs. or 1.5 to 2.5 kg.)
1 lb. (500 g.) chestnuts. Broth or bouillon
1 cooked chicken liver, chopped
2 tablespoons butter or margarine. 2 eggs, beaten
2 tablespoons cream. 2 truffles, chopped
1 tablespoon lemon juice. 2 tablespoons snipped parsley
Nutmeg, sage to taste. 4 tablespoons butter, melted
1 glass red wine
½ cup (115 g. or about ¼ pt.) thick sour cream

Rub chicken inside and out with *salt* and *pepper*.
Slit shells of chestnuts crosswise and spread on baking sheet. Roast in a very hot oven (450°F or 230°C) until shells pop open. Remove shells and inner skins. Cook chestnuts in broth until soft enough to force through a coarse sieve or food mill. Combine chestnut purée with chicken livers, 2 tablespoons butter, eggs, cream, chopped truffles, lemon juice, parsley and seasonings. Fill chicken with stuffing; close body cavity with skewers and cord. Fasten wings and legs to the body with cord.
Put chicken into a deep saucepot and brush with melted butter. Brown slowly on all sides. Add wine and just enough boiling *water* to cover bottom of pot. Cover and cook 1½ hours, basting frequently with liquid in skillet. Remove chicken to a heated platter and keep warm. If needed, add hot water to saucepot and bring to boiling, stirring and scraping bottom to loosen drippings. Blend in sour cream and season to taste. If necessary thicken gravy with *2 teaspoons (6 g.) cornstarch* mixed with several tablespoons *cold water*. Garnish platter with *grapes* and serve chicken with *Brussels sprouts*.
4 to 6 servings

Canard à l'Orange
France

This classic French recipe for roast duck calls especially for a young duck (duckling); so, instead of canard, the specialty should have been named Caneton à l'Orange. The flavor of roast duck and orange complement each other perfectly, a fact well known to gourmets. The following recipe suggests a stuffing of orange and apple slices. The roast duckling may be garnished with canned mandarin oranges and the syrup from can used to make the sauce. Or one may garnish with orange slices brushed with melted butter and lightly browned under the broiler or in a skillet over direct heat.

1 duckling, 4 to 5 lbs. (1¾ to 2¼ kg.)
Salt, pepper, thyme. 2 oranges, pared and sliced
2 apples, cored and sliced
1 bay leaf, crushed. Chopped parsley
Juice of two large oranges
1 tablespoon butter or margarine, melted
1 glass dry white wine. 7 teaspoons (20 g.) cornstarch

Rub cavity of duckling with salt, pepper and thyme. Stuff with a mixture of the sliced oranges and apples, crushed bay leaf and parsley. To close cavity, sew or skewer and lace with cord.

Place duckling on a rack in roasting pan and set in a slow oven (325°F or 160°C). Roast about 2½ hours, basting frequently with a blend of ½ cup (⅛ liter) of the orange juice and the melted butter. Spoon off the fat occasionally from roasting pan into a bowl. When duckling is tender and well browned, remove to a heated platter and keep warm. If needed, return some of the drippings in bowl to roasting pan. Add the wine and remaining orange juice. Bring to boiling, stirring to loosen drippings from bottom of pan. Add very finely cut *strips of orange peel* and mix well. Thicken the sauce with cornstarch blended with several tablespoons *cold water,* cooking and stirring until smooth. Pour sauce into a gravy boat.

Garnish the roast duckling with *mandarin orange sections* or with *orange slices* broiled with *butter.*
4 servings

11

Cannelloni
Italy

Cannelloni is a pasta or thin pancake rolled up with a ground meat and vegetable stuffing. If desired, a mixture of leftover meat, including sausage, can be used in the stuffing. Both pancake and pasta recipes are included.

¾ cup (100 g. or 3½ oz.) flour. ¼ teaspoon salt
3 medium eggs, slightly beaten
6 tablespoons water. Olive oil
½ lb. (250 g.) ground meat
½ lb. (250 g.) fresh spinach, finely chopped
2 tablespoons chopped onion. ½ teaspoon salt
½ teaspoon oregano. Fine dry bread crumbs
1 egg, slightly beaten. Tomato purée
Butter or margarine. Grated Parmesan or Romano cheese

Prepare a smooth pancake batter combining the flour, salt, eggs and water. Let batter rest for 2 hours. To make pancakes, pour batter from a pitcher or end of tablespoon onto lightly greased hot griddle, forming thin 4 to 5 inch (10 to 13 centimeter) rounds. Bake over medium heat until lightly browned on both sides. Keep pancakes warm.
Heat several tablespoons olive oil in a large skillet. Add meat, spinach, onion, salt and oregano; cook, stirring occasionally, until browned. Set aside to cool slightly. Add bread crumbs, egg and enough tomato purée to moisten. Mix thoroughly and spread mixture over pancakes. Roll them up and place, side by side, in greased baking dish. Dot with butter and sprinkle with cheese. Heat in a hot oven (425°F or 220°C) 12 to 15 minutes, or until lightly browned.
About 4 servings

Variation: Substitute pasta squares for the pancakes. Combine *1 cup (115 grams or 4 ounces) flour* with *1 egg* plus *1 egg yolk, 1 tablespoon water,* a little *olive oil* and *¼ teaspoon salt.* Knead the dough thoroughly until smooth. Let rest 1 hour. Roll out very thin and cut into 3½-inch (9-centimeter) squares. Drop into *boiling salted water* to which *1 teaspoon olive oil* has been added. Cook about 8 minutes. Remove squares with slotted spoon and place on a cloth to dry. Proceed as directed.

12

Carbonada Criolla
Argentina

The cuisine of the Latin American Creoles, descendants of the conquistadores, enjoys an excellent reputation throughout the American continent. The mother of Creole cooking is French; its father is Spanish. And with the passing of time, it is possible to discern the tutelage of Indians and the magic touch of Africans, whose lively genius was revealed in the kitchen. At first glance, the combination of ingredients in this Creole dish might seem strange, but the delicious results will be pleasantly surprising. The dish is usually served in a pumpkin shell.

2 lbs. (1 kg.) veal, cut in pieces
Flour, salt. Lard for frying
2 garlic cloves, crushed. 2 medium onions, chopped
2 green peppers, cut in strips
3 medium tomatoes, cut in wedges
Soup greens (see note with Bollito Misto)
1 cup (100 g. or 3½ oz.) chopped celery; or
use celery root (celeriac)
1½ teaspoons salt. 6 peppercorns
¼ to ½ teaspoon cayenne pepper. 1 bay leaf
½ teaspoon thyme. ¼ teaspoon marjoram
4 tablespoons chopped parsley
1 cup (¼ liter or about ½ pt.) white wine
2 cups (½ liter or about 1 pt.) broth or bouillon
4 potatoes, pared and cubed
½ lb. (250 g.) pumpkin meat, cubed
2 apples, pared and cut in wedges
1 small can whole kernel corn, drained
2 peaches, peeled and cut in wedges
½ lb. (250 g.) grapes. Fluffy hot rice

Coat veal with a mixture of flour and salt and brown well in hot lard in a large saucepot.
Lightly brown the garlic, onion, green pepper and tomato in hot lard in a skillet. Add to the meat with soup greens and celery. Add seasonings, wine and broth; cover and simmer about 1 hour. Add potato, pumpkin and apple and cook 15 minutes. Add corn, peaches and grapes; heat only to serving temperature. Add seasoning, if needed. Just before serving add hot rice; or serve rice separately. Serve in a hollowed-out pumpkin.
About 10 servings

Cassoulet
France

It appears that the cities of Castelnaudary, Toulouse and Carcasonne in the Languedoc region still fight for the honor of having first created this nourishing bean dish. Every housewife keeps the ingredients and seasonings of her Cassoulet variant a secret. This much is certain: the dish must include white beans and meat among its ingredients. The meat combination is often mutton with either goose or duckling.

1 lb. (500 g.) dried white beans (navy or Great Northern)
1 to 2 teaspoons salt. 2 garlic cloves, minced
¼ lb. (125 g.) smoked bacon (or salt pork)
1 garlic-flavored sausage. Lard or other shortening
½ lb. (250 g.) pork shoulder, diced
½ lb. (250 g.) mutton, cut in cubes
2 medium onions, chopped. 1 bay leaf
Soup greens (see note with Bollito Misto), chopped
1 small can tomato purée. Salt, pepper, thyme
Coarse dry bread crumbs. Butter or margarine

Soak beans in about *6 cups (1½ liters) water* in a saucepot. The next day add salt and just enough water to cover beans; add garlic, bacon and sausage. Bring to boiling.
In a skillet, brown cubed meat in several tablespoons lard along with onion, bay leaf and soup greens. Add to the saucepot. Stir in tomato purée and season mixture with salt, pepper and thyme. Cover and cook gently until meat and beans are tender (about 2 hours). Remove bacon and sausage; slice and return to beans.
Turn mixture into an ovenproof casserole; cover with bread crumbs; dot with butter and set in a hot oven (400°F or 200°C) 10 minutes, or until well browned. (Or, if desired, brown crumbs under broiler heat.) Fold under the crusty surface; sprinkle again with crumbs; dot with butter and return to oven to brown; repeat this procedure.
About 6 servings

14

Cevapcici
Yugoslavia

These savory sausage-shaped meat rolls originated in Yugoslavia, but similar versions are served in neighboring countries. Depending on the country of origin, the meat rolls are made of a single meat (beef or lamb) or a combination (beef and veal or pork, or equal portions of beef, lamb and pork). Cevapcici are at their best grilled over an open fire.

1 lb. (500 g.) ground lean beef
1 lb. (500 g.) ground lean pork
1 teaspoon salt. ¼ teaspoon pepper
1 teaspoon paprika. 1 egg, slightly beaten
1 large garlic clove, crushed
5 or 6 drops Tabasco. 1 teaspoon marjoram
3 to 4 tablespoons beef broth or bouillon

Combine all ingredients in a mixing bowl. Lightly knead mixture to blend thoroughly. Form into finger-shaped sausages about ¾ inch (2 centimeters) thick and 4 inches (10 centimeters) long. Cook slowly until well browned on a charcoal grill or under a broiler about 5 inches (13 centimeters) from the heat. Turn sausages often as they cook. They are done when brown on outside and slightly pink inside.

According to Yugoslavian tradition, these little sausages are served with coarsely chopped onion, tiny hot peppers, bread and a popular plum brandy called Slivovitz.
About 6 servings

Note: If desired, impale the rolls, side by side and slightly separated, on skewers for grilling; serve on skewers or remove from skewers before serving. Or, fry the rolls in a heavy skillet containing a small amount of lard heated to the smoking point; turn occasionally using a wide spatula.

15

Charlotte Russe
Soviet Union

The word charlotte as used nowadays refers to many types of cold molded dishes, usually desserts that are prepared in molds lined with ladyfingers, sponge cake, wafer-type cookies, or even thin bread slices. The fillings include rich creamy custard, gelatin and whipped cream mixtures, fruit combinations with whipped cream and many others. Here is a popular version using ladyfingers and a rich Bavarian cream-like filling. French gourmets maintain that Charlotte Russe was created, not by a Russian, but by the famous French cook, Antoine Carême, and so should be called Charlotte Parisienne.

60 ladyfingers, separated in halves
1 pkg. (3¾ oz.) chocolate pudding and pie filling mix
2 cups (½ liter or about 1 pt.) milk
2 eggs, separated. ½ cup sugar
1 tablespoon vanilla-flavored sugar
2 teaspoons instant coffee
3 oz. (85 g.) unsweetened chocolate
3 env. (3 oz.) unflavored gelatin
2 to 3 teaspoons brandy
3 oz. (85 g.) blanched almonds, chopped
1 cup (¼ liter or about ½ pt.) heavy cream, whipped

Place the rim of a 9-inch (23-centimeter) springform pan on a cake plate; cut ladyfingers straight at one end so they will stand upright in pan. Arrange them around inside of rim, rounded side out.
Mix chocolate pudding with 1 cup of the milk in a heavy saucepan. Stir in egg yolks and remaining 1 cup of milk. Add sugar mixed with instant coffee. Stir over low heat until boiling. Add the chocolate (cut in pieces) and heat until chocolate is melted and mixture is smooth, stirring constantly. Meanwhile, soften gelatin in 1½ cups (⅜ liter or about ¾ pint) cold milk in a saucepan. Heat only until gelatin is dissolved. Blend into chocolate mixture; add brandy and nuts. Fold in egg whites, stiffly beaten. Chill until slightly thickened. Reserving some of the whipped cream for decorating, fold remainder into chocolate mixture. Fill pan with alternate layers of ladyfingers and chocolate mixture. Also use the cut-off ends of ladyfingers. Chill until firm. When ready to serve, decorate with additional ladyfingers, whipped cream and candied cherries.
8 to 10 servings

Chateaubriand
France

Many writers, intrigued by François René Vicomte de Chateaubriand (1768-1848), wrote novels based on his stormy life. The Vicomte began his career as an officer in the French army. During the French Revolution, he traveled among the American Indians. Returning to France, he entered the diplomatic service, but soon left it because his opinions differed from those of Napoleon. After the downfall of Napoleon, Chateaubriand was nominated peer of France, represented his country in Berlin and London and finally became head of the foreign ministry. Three things made him famous: the several changes in his political thinking, his long attachment to Madame de Recamier, and the Chateaubriand, created by his cook, Montmireil. Originally, the Chateaubriand was a fillet of beef, slit at the side and filled with a delicious stuffing. Nowadays, Chateaubriand refers to a thick fillet that weighs about one pound and is taken from the center of the beef tenderloin. The meat is usually grilled or broiled and served with any of the various sauces used to complement steak.

**1 lb. (500 g.) Chateaubriand (steak cut from
thickest part of tenderloin)
Shortening. Salt, pepper**

Brown meat on all sides in hot shortening in a heavy skillet, about 15 to 20 minutes, turning occasionally. Or, if desired, place the meat on greased rack in broiler pan and broil about 5 inches (about 13 centimeters) from heat until meat is well browned outside and pink and juicy inside, turning to brown all sides. Keep warm and let rest 10 minutes before slicing; season.

Serve the meat on a preheated platter surrounded by French fried potatoes, grilled tomatoes, mushrooms, peas, carrots and white asparagus. Serve with sauce Béarnaise, if desired.
About 2 servings

17

Cheesecake
United States

Even the ancient Greeks knew some form of cheesecake. There are probably more theories about the making of cheesecake than there are people who know how to bake it. Cheesecake, as served today, usually refers to a creamy cake made of one or more cheeses such as cream cheese or cottage cheese (sometimes called curds), with eggs, milk or cream and various flavorings added. A cheesecake may be baked like a pie in a pastry or crumb crust, while other cheesecakes require no baking and often contain gelatin. The following is a version which is as easy to prepare as it is delightful to eat.

9 slices or 70 g. zwieback, coarsely crushed
(about 1 cup crumbs)
⅔ cup (135 g. or about 5 oz.) sugar
4 tablespoons (50 g. or 2 oz.) butter or margarine
1 lb. (500 g.) cream cheese. 1 teaspoon grated lemon peel
1 tablespoon lemon juice. 5 eggs, separated

Place zwieback between layers of waxed paper or aluminum foil and crush with rolling pin; mix with 2 teaspoons of the sugar and the butter. Work with your hands until ingredients are blended well. Put zwieback into a 9-inch (23-centimeter) springform pan and press firmly on bottom, using back of tablespoon.

Soften the cream cheese and beat in remaining sugar, a small amount at a time; beat in lemon peel, lemon juice and egg yolks. Continue beating until fluffy.

Beat egg whites until stiff peaks are formed. Gently fold into cream cheese mixture until thoroughly blended. Turn mixture into pan over zwieback crust and bake in a slow oven (300°F or 150°C) about 75 minutes, or until filling is "set." Remove from oven and cool on a rack about 10 minutes before removing rim from springform pan. Allow cheesecake to rest about 3 hours before serving.

8 to 10 servings

Chicory Salad
Belgium

In Belgium, chicory (better known to Americans as Belgian or French endive) is served almost daily, usually in salads with a vinegar and oil dressing, with Flemish Dressing or with commercially available dressing. Chicory, as it is grown in Belgium, is a tightly folded plant that grows upright in a thin stalk with narrow tapering leaves. It is generally bleached white while growing. Chicory has been known for centuries: the Greeks and Romans were said to have used it as a healing herb. Many small farms near Brussels grow this delicate, leafy vegetable almost exclusively, providing the farmers with a very good living. Here is a tossed salad combination often served in Belgium.

1 lb. (500 g.) Belgian endive. 2 tomatoes
½ lb. (250 g.) Swiss cheese (in a piece)
4 hard-cooked eggs. 3 tablespoons vinegar
1 tablespoon lemon juice. 3 tablespoons salad oil
1 teaspoon dry mustard. Salt, pepper, sugar to taste

Rinse chicory thoroughly and cut off bottom of stalk. If desired, immerse a few seconds in lukewarm water to eliminate bitterness. Dry thoroughly. Divide stalk lengthwise into quarters or eighths (depending on size of stalk). Remove skin from tomatoes and cut into wedges. Cut the cheese into narrow strips. Cut each egg into 8 wedges. Put all these ingredients into a salad bowl. Blend vinegar, lemon juice, oil and other seasonings. Pour dressing over salad. Chill about 30 minutes before serving.
4 servings
Flemish Dressing
Mash *2 hard-cooked egg yolks;* add *2 to 3 teaspoons grated onion, 1 garlic clove, crushed, 1 teaspoon chopped chervil, 3 tablespoons olive oil, 1 tablespoon vinegar* or *lemon juice* and *salt* and *pepper* to taste. Beat until thoroughly blended, then mix in *½ cup (⅛ liter* or *about ¼ pint)* cream. Pour dressing on salad and toss until dressing coats salad.

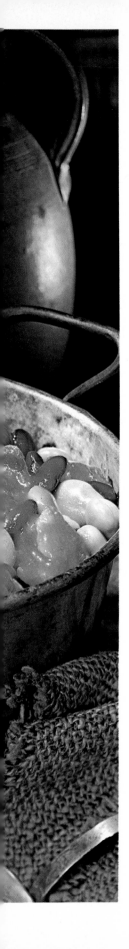

Chili Con Carne
Mexico

Chili (or chile) is the Latin American word for a hot pepper; thus Chili con Carne means peppers with meat. Originating in Mexico, the dish has become popular in the United States, especially in the southwestern states. There are many versions of this dish, but its main ingredients are beef, tomato (or tomato sauce), beans and chili peppers, for which chili powder is often substituted. The following recipe contains both beef and pork.

1 can white beans, drained. 1 can kidney beans, drained
1 lb. (500 g.) beef, cut up. 1 lb. (500 g.) pork, cut up
4 tablespoons lard
1 cup (¼ liter or about ½ pt.) beef broth or bouillon
¼ to ½ teaspoon caraway seed (optional)
1 teaspoon salt
1 to 2 tablespoons chili powder; or use
1 to 2 hot chili peppers. 2 garlic cloves, crushed
1 large onion, chopped. 3 tomatoes, peeled and cut up

If dried pinto (or red) beans are used instead of canned ones, wash and soak them overnight; then cook them slowly until tender, about 2 hours.

Brown meat in hot lard in a Dutch oven or heavy saucepot; add broth; cover and cook gently until meat is about half done. Add caraway seed (if used), salt, chili powder and garlic. Continue cooking until meat is tender; add beans.

Meanwhile, heat several tablespoons *lard* in a skillet; add onion, tomatoes and peppers (if used); cover and let simmer until vegetables are soft. Force through a sieve and thicken with *cornstarch* (mixed with *cold water* before adding). Stir thickened sauce into meat and beans. Blend well. Cook over low heat until thoroughly heated. Add more seasoning, if needed.

About 6 servings

Chop Suey
United States, China

The Chinese influence is apparent in many aspects of this dish: the careful cutting of the ingredients into small pieces; the use of soy sauce and ginger; the rapid cooking of meat and vegetables for a very short time, that is characteristic of Chinese cuisine. Chop Suey can be prepared very tastily. However, it is not a Chinese dish as one might think, but an invention of Chinese cooks living in the United States. Although Chinese cook books never include Chop Suey, it enjoys great popularity in many countries where one will find interesting variations of the recipe.

½ lb. (250 g.) cooked boneless pork
1¾ cups (250 g. or ½ lb.) cut-up cooked chicken
½ lb. (250 g.) fresh mushrooms
Peanut oil or other cooking oil
½ lb. (250 g.) canned sliced bamboo shoots, drained
1 cup (100 g. or 3½ oz.) diagonally sliced celery
8 green onions (or leeks), cut in pieces
1 cup (¼ liter or about ½ pt.) chicken broth
2 cloves garlic, crushed. ½ teaspoon salt
⅛ teaspoon pepper. 2 teaspoons sugar
3 to 4 teaspoons soy sauce. ⅛ teaspoon ground ginger
3 tablespoons sherry. 1 tablespoon (9 g.) cornstarch

Cut pork and chicken into strips; slice mushrooms lengthwise through stems and caps. Sauté these ingredients one after the other in hot oil in a heavy skillet or saucepot, turning frequently. (Vegetables should be crisp-tender; do not overcook.)
Return pork, bamboo shoots, celery and onion to skillet. Set aside mushrooms and chicken. Add chicken broth and garlic to skillet. Season with salt, pepper and sugar. Cover and bring rapidly to boiling. Combine soy sauce, ginger and sherry. Add cornstarch that has been mixed with several tablespoons *cold broth* or *water*. Stir into hot mixture; cook and stir until thickened. Add chicken and mushrooms and continue cooking only until heated through. Serve with fluffy rice or Chinese noodles.
About 4 servings

Clam Chowder
United States

Clam Chowder, a thick appetite-satisfying soup, is a specialty of America's New England states. The original recipe goes back to the early settlers who had to make do with whatever food was available in the new land. Since fish and shellfish were plentiful, they were used from the beginning in many of the old regional recipes. It is a known fact that clam chowder fanciers are divided into two factions. New Englanders insist upon milk or cream and potatoes in their chowder while New Yorkers and many other gourmets around the country prefer Manhattan chowder which includes tomatoes among its ingredients.

Here is our recipe which has New York and New England overtones as it includes potatoes, tomatoes and celery among its ingredients.

6 slices (100 g. or 3½ oz.) bacon, diced
2 onions, chopped. 1 green pepper, cut in slivers
Soup greens (see note with Bollito Misto)
3 cups (¾ liter or about 1½ pts.) broth (bouillon) or
use clam broth, if available
2 small potatoes, pared and diced
2 medium tomatoes, peeled and cut up
1 cup (100 g. or 3½ oz.) sliced celery
1 can (8 oz. or 225 g.) minced clams, drained; reserve
liquid (or cook fresh hard-shelled clams and
reserve the broth)
Salt. Cayenne pepper
4 tablespoons thick sour cream. 2 egg yolks

In a heavy saucepot, combine the bacon with chopped onion, green pepper and soup greens. Cook over medium heat, stirring occasionally until bacon is browned; add broth (or broth and clam liquid), potato, tomato and celery. Cook over low heat about 30 minutes or until vegetables are tender. Add clams and season to taste. Combine sour cream and egg yolks. Stir into hot chowder. Serve at once.
About 6 servings

Crêpes Suzette
France

Crêpes Suzette is a French term for a dessert consisting of very thin pancakes rolled up and served with a sauce and flambéed at the table. It is said that this French specialty was created in honor of a lady named Suzette. The story goes that Edward VII, Prince of Wales and later King of England, had secret rendezvous in a quiet restaurant with Suzette, a Parisian midinette. So, the cook of the restaurant created crêpes with orange sauce for Suzette. A romantic myth perhaps, but charming!

1 cup (115 g. or 4 oz.) flour. ¼ teaspoon salt
1 tablespoon confectioners' sugar
¾ cup (175 ml. or about ⅓ pt.) milk
3 eggs, slightly beaten. Dash rum
Shortening. 2 oranges, grated peel and juice
10 lumps sugar. 4 to 6 tablespoons butter or margarine
1 to 2 small glasses Grand Marnier
2 small glasses maraschino. Slivered almonds, toasted

Prepare a batter of the flour, salt, confectioners' sugar, milk, eggs and rum; let rest about 30 minutes.

Lightly grease a 6-inch (15-centimeter) skillet. Heat to moderately hot. Spoon about 2 tablespoons batter into the skillet and tilt back and forth to spread batter thinly and evenly. Cook each crêpe until lightly browned on both sides. Fold crêpes in quarters and keep warm.

Sprinkle grated peel over sugar lumps. Melt butter in a clean skillet. Stir in orange juice slowly; add sugar lumps, heat and stir until sugar is dissolved. Blend in Grand Marnier and place the folded crêpes in the sauce. Spoon some of the sauce over the crêpes and let rest several minutes. Pour maraschino over the crêpes and ignite. Serve very hot sprinkled with toasted almonds.

4 to 6 servings

Culbastija
Yugoslavia

According to Yugoslavian tradition this dish is made with pork chops, but it is just as flavorful made with any other tender cut of meat.

Culbastija is a modernized version of roast on the spit which, in Yugoslavia, is the culinary highlight of a picnic or a vintage festival. The fireplace is improvised; two fork branches are stuck into the ground to hold a spit that has a rotating device at one end. A hole, in which a charcoal fire is ignited, is dug underneath the spit. Only when the fire is burned down and reduced to glowing charcoal can the roasting begin. If the roast tends to brown too rapidly, the heat is controlled by throwing ashes onto the glowing coals. During the roasting, the meat is brushed frequently with shortening or oil until a firm crust has formed. The roast must remain juicy and pink inside.

If necessary, cook Culbastija under a broiler, but for best results follow directions for grilling over an open fire.

2 lbs. (1 kg.) pork loin
2 tablespoons cooking oil
Salt, pepper. 2 onions, finely chopped

Cut pork into 8 chops; pound them lightly with meat hammer and brush with oil. Place on grill over open fire and cook slowly until well browned on both sides; season to taste. Arrange the chops on a preheated platter and cover with chopped onion. Serve with fresh tomato salad, bread and wine.

4 to 6 servings

24

Duvede
Yugoslavia

This meal-in-a-dish is known by similar names in all the Balkan countries.

1 lb. (500 g.) lean pork
1 lb. (500 g.) lean lamb or beef
2 tomatoes, sliced. 2 green peppers, sliced
2 small eggplants, pared and sliced
1 garlic clove, crushed
1 medium onion, chopped. Parsley
¼ teaspoon salt. ¼ teaspoon pepper. Paprika

5 tablespoons olive oil
2 cups (400 g. or 14 oz.) cooked rice
6 oz. (170 g.) Chedder cheese, shredded

Slice meat about ¼ inch thick. Arrange in a large casserole alternating layers of meat with vegetable slices. Sprinkle each layer with a mixture of garlic, onion and parsley. Season with salt, pepper and paprika. Pour a little oil over the layers.

Cover casserole and place in a 350°F (180°C) oven about 1½ hours, or until meat is tender. Uncover and top with rice; sprinkle with cheese and a little oil. Return to oven until cheese is melted. Sprinkle with paprika and garnish with parsley sprigs.   *6 to 8 servings*

25

Dolmas
Turkey

Dolmas are vegetables (eggplant, green pepper, cabbage or grape leaves) with a stuffing of well seasoned ground lamb, rice and onion.

4 green peppers. Olive oil. 1 onion, chopped
¾ lb. (350 g.) ground lamb
1½ cups (300 g. or 10 oz.) cooked rice
Salt. Pepper. ¼ teaspoon oregano
¼ teaspoon cumin seed
2 cups (½ liter or about 1 pt.) broth

3 tablespoons tomato paste. Lemon juice
2 teaspoons (6 grams) cornstarch
½ cup (115 g. or ¼ pt.) thick sour cream

Cut tops from peppers, remove seeds and fiber; rinse and dry peppers. Brown onion and meat in several tablespoons oil in a skillet. Mix with rice and seasonings. Stuff peppers; brush shells with oil. Sauté peppers in hot oil in a heatproof casserole. Add broth; cover and cook gently until peppers are just tender. Stir tomato paste into broth; add lemon juice and seasoning to taste. Blend cornstarch with sour cream and stir into sauce. Cook gently until sauce is thickened.
4 servings

26

Empanadas
Chile

These delicious meat pies are closely related to Russian Piroshki. It is customary in Chile to prepare the empanadas with hot spices. The saying goes that, ''empanadas must burn''—either with red pepper or chopped chilis.

4½ cups (500 g. or about 1 lb.) flour
½ teaspoon baking powder. ½ teaspoon salt
1 cup (200 g. or 8 oz.) butter, chilled
2 eggs, slightly beaten. 8 tablespoons lukewarm milk
Filling
2 to 3 tablespoons oil
½ lb. (250 g.) ground pork (or half beef)
1 large garlic clove, crushed. ½ cup finely chopped onion
⅓ cup finely chopped celery
2 large ripe tomatoes, peeled and chopped
⅓ cup (50 g. or 2 oz.) raisins, chopped
8 pimento-stuffed olives, finely chopped
½ teaspoon salt. 1 teaspoon sugar
1 canned small hot chili, minced; or
½ teaspoon chopped dried chili
¼ teaspoon marjoram leaves. ¼ teaspoon paprika
2 hard-cooked eggs, finely chopped
Shortening, heated to 365-375°F (185-190°C)

Mix flour with baking powder and salt in a mixing bowl; cut in half of the butter, using a pastry blender or two knives. Add a mixture of eggs and milk, mixing only until dough can be formed into a ball. Turn onto a lightly floured pastry canvas and roll into a rectangle. Cut remaining chilled fat into small pieces and distribute over surface of dough. Fold dough over several times; knead gently until very smooth and easy to handle, using as little flour on canvas as necessary. Form into a ball. Wrap well and chill several hours or overnight.

To prepare filling, heat oil in a skillet; add meat and next 3 ingredients; cook and stir about 5 minutes, or until meat is browned. Add tomato and cook 3 minutes. Mix in remaining ingredients, except shortening.

Roll out dough (half at a time) until very thin; cut into 4-inch rounds. Spoon 1 heaped tablespoon of filling on each; brush edges with slightly beaten *egg white* and press to seal. Deep-fry empanadas in hot fat until golden on both sides.
About 4 dozen empanadas

Enchiladas
Mexico

An enchilada is a tortilla (or pancake), rolled up and filled with a meat, chicken, or cheese mixture. In Latin American countries, tortillas are usually prepared with corn flour or corn meal. Mexican women are masters of the art of kneading masa (corn flour dough) and flattening it with their hands to form the thin tortillas. Tortillas are time-consuming to prepare; if frozen or canned tortillas are not available at your supermarket, try the recipe below, which uses pancakes made with regular flour instead of corn flour.

2¼ cups (250 g. or 9 oz.) flour. ¼ teaspoon salt
4 eggs. 2 cups (½ liter or about 1 pt.) milk
Shortening or oil. 1 to 2 teaspoons chili powder
1 teaspoon paprika. ¼ teaspoon pepper
1 onion, finely chopped. 1 large garlic clove, crushed
2 tablespoons finely minced parsley
4 tomatoes, peeled and cut up
1 tablespoon tomato ketchup
½ lb. (250 g. or 9 oz.) cooked ham, chopped
½ teaspoon marjoram. ¼ teaspoon cayenne pepper
¼ lb. (100 g. or 4 oz.) sliced Cheddar cheese,
cut in strips

Prepare pancake batter using the flour, salt, 3 of the eggs and 1⅓ cups (315 milliliters) of the milk. Beat until smooth and set aside 1 hour. Pour onto a hot, lightly greased skillet, forming a large thin pancake. Brown lightly on both sides. Repeat with remaining batter.
Mix remaining milk with the egg and season with chili powder, paprika and pepper. Dip pancakes into mixture and return to hot skillet to brown well on both sides. Keep warm. Combine in a saucepan the onion, garlic, parsley, tomato and ketchup; cook 3 minutes. Add the ham, marjoram and cayenne pepper. Simmer until thickened. Spoon mixture onto the pancakes and roll up; place them in a greased baking dish. Top with cheese and heat in a moderate oven (350°F or 180°C) until the cheese is melted. Serve hot with a lettuce salad.
7 or 8 large enchiladas

Strawberries Romanoff
Soviet Union

The taste-tempting secret of this delightful dessert is that the strawberries have been marinated in orange juice and curaçao (or Cointreau) before they are served with sweetened whipped cream. A variation of this dessert, called Coupe Romanoff, includes vanilla ice cream among its ingredients. No one is certain how this dessert came about. It is named for the Russian Romanov (sometimes spelled Romanoff) dynasty, from which came all Russian rulers from 1613 to 1917. The most important Romanov was Tsar Peter the Great. It is quite possible that this strawberry specialty goes back to his time. He certainly appreciated good food and above all, good drink.

1½ pts. (500 g.) ripe strawberries
2 to 3 tablespoons sugar. 2 tablespoons curaçao
1 large orange, juice and grated peel
1 cup (¼ litre or about ½ pt.) heavy cream
Vanilla-flavored sugar

Rinse and hull the strawberries; dry thoroughly. Combine in a bowl with a mixture of sugar, curaçao, orange juice and grated peel. Pour over berries and refrigerate several hours.
Beat heavy cream in a chilled bowl until soft peaks are formed. Beat in several tablespoons vanilla-flavored sugar until stiff peaks are formed. Put alternate layers of strawberries and sweetened whipped cream in glasses or bowls. Chill before serving.
4 servings

Variations: Place in each serving dish a scoop of *vanilla ice cream.* Arrange marinated *strawberries* over it and garnish with *whipped cream.*
For a refreshing purée-type dessert to serve in tall glasses, blend about *two-thirds* of the *marinated strawberries* and *3* or *4 scoops* of *vanilla ice cream* in an electric blender until of pouring consistency. Turn into glasses and garnish with remaining *strawberries* and dollops of *whipped cream.*

Beef
à la Esterházy
Hungary

The Esterházys of Galantha were Hungarian magnates who in 1687 rose to the princely rank. Their estate, consisting of 21 castles, 60 hamlets, and 414 villages, was still the largest estate in Hungary in 1945. The most famous members of the family were Nikolaus Joseph (1714-1790) who had built the castle in Esterháza in which Haydn worked for 30 years as a music conductor; and Nikolaus, Prince of Esterházy (1765-1833), the renowned Austro-Hungarian Field Marshal who could afford to refuse the Hungarian Crown that Napoleon offered to him in 1809. It is believed that the latter is the man for whom this dish is named.

1¾ lbs. (750 g.) beef top loin. Lard or other shortening
Salt. Pepper. Paprika
Soup greens (see note with Bollito Misto)
1 medium onion. 1 tablespoon flour
1 cup (¼ liter or about ½ pt.) broth or bouillon
1 tablespoon lemon juice. Dash Madeira
½ cup (115 g. or about ¼ pt.) thick sour cream

Brush meat with hot lard or other shortening; brown on all sides on the grill. Season with salt, pepper, and paprika.
Clean and chop the soup greens and onion. Brown lightly in a small amount of fat in a skillet. Sprinkle with the flour and stir until blended. Gradually add the broth, cooking and stirring until mixture comes to boiling. Add the meat and finish cooking together with the vegetables. Remove meat and strain the sauce into a saucepan; add the lemon juice, wine, and sour cream. Blend well and season to taste. Add sliced meat to the sauce. Serve with spätzle or mashed potatoes.
About 6 servings

30

Fondue Bourguignonne
Switzerland

Fondue is a Swiss creation, although the word actually comes from the French verb *fondre*, meaning "to melt". One usually associates the word fondue with the classic Swiss dish made of cheese. Fondue Bourguignonne, however, is a meat dish in which small cubes of beef are speared on long forks and cooked to taste in very hot oil, then dipped into a well-seasoned sauce and eaten piping hot. The dish is supposed to have been introduced by the Burgundians who, in 1476 under Charles the Bold, occupied the western part of Switzerland.

> 2 lbs. (1 kg.) beef tenderloin, cut in small cubes
> Vegetable shortening or sunflower oil for deep frying

Prepare the meat cubes and put them into a serving bowl. Heat shortening or oil in the fondue pot until very hot. Spear meat with fondue fork and deep-fry in the hot oil until browned. Serve meat with various sauces.

6 to 8 servings

Sauce suggestions:

Chili Onion Sauce. Combine *½ envelope (about ¾ ounce or 20 grams) dry onion soup mix* and *¾ cup (175 milliliters) boiling water* in a saucepan. Cook 10 minutes. Add gradually, *1½ tablespoons (10 grams) flour* mixed with *¼ cup (60 milliliters)* water. Cook and stir until boiling; continue cooking until sauce is thickened. Mix in *2 to 3 tablespoons* chili sauce.

Cream Cheese Horseradish Sauce. Soften *4½ ounces (125 grams) cream cheese* and blend in *4 tablespoons (60 milliliters) milk, 2 tablespoons grated horseradish, 1 teaspoon Worcestershire sauce,* and *salt* to taste.

Curry Sauce 1. Blend *1 teaspoon curry powder* with *⅔ cup (125 grams or ¼ pint) mayonnaise, 2 teaspoons evaporated milk, 1 teaspoon red currant jelly, ½ teaspoon sugar* and a *dash lemon juice.*

Curry Sauce 2. Blend *1 tablespoon curry powder* with *1 cup (200 grams or about ½ pint) mayonnaise, 1 teaspoon grated onion* and *½ teaspoon lemon juice.*

Mayonnaise Horseradish Sauce. Blend *2 tablespoons prepared horseradish, 1 teaspoon grated onion* and *½ teaspoon lemon juice* with *1 cup (200 grams or about ½ pint) mayonnaise.*

31

Fondue Neuchâteloise
Switzerland

1 garlic clove
6 tablespoons dry white wine (Neuchâtel)
¾ lb. (300 g.) each Swiss cheese and
Gruyère cheese
5 teaspoons (15 g.) cornstarch
1 small glass kirsch
Salt. Pepper. Nutmeg

The classic Swiss fondue is a dish of melted cheese or a combination of several cheeses seasoned with a variety of ingredients. To eat fondue, each individual spears a small piece of French bread or crusty roll on a long-handled fork, then dips the bread into the hot fondue mixture and eats it immediatelely.

Rub fondue pot of casserole with clove of garlic; pour in the wine and heat; shred cheese, add and heat to a creamy consistency, stirring constantly. Mix cornstarch with kirsch and add it to the cheese when cheese starts to bubble. Season to taste. Place pot on an alcohol burner on a metal tray at the table. Serve with hot tea, wine or kirsch.
About 6 servings

32

Trout with Almonds
Switzerland

A witty gourmet once said that this is a dish for a cardinal, not a king, because cardinals know more about food.

4 trout. Salt. Lemon juice. Flour. Shortening
1 glass red wine. 2 teaspoons (6 g.) cornstarch
3½ oz. (100 g.) slivered almonds

Prepare trout; sprinkle with salt and lemon juice. Let rest for a few minutes, then carefully pat dry. Dredge fish with flour. Brown in hot shortening in a skillet until golden on all sides. Arrange on a preheated platter. Add wine to drippings and bring to boiling. Stir in cornstarch mixed with a little *wine* or *water*. Season to taste and cook until thickened and smooth. Lightly brown almonds in a small amount of *butter*, sprinkle over trout and pour the sauce over all. Serve with *lemon slices* and *lettuce salad*.
4 Servings

33

Gefillte Fish (Stuffed Whole Fish)
Israel

This is the famous dish of the eastern Jews, prepared for the evening before the Sabbath. It is time-consuming in its preparation, but your efforts will be rewarded. The unique method used in this recipe—combining the fish and other ingredients to be stuffed in a fish skin—has the advantage of no one having to struggle with bones while at the table. Besides, less attractive types of fish can be transformed into epicurean creations. However, should the preparation described be too complicated, simply shape the stuffing into balls and simmer them in the hot fish broth, a method often used to prepare Gefillte Fish.

2 tenches (or small carp). Salt. Lemon juice
Soup greens (see note with Bollito Misto)
6 tablespoons butter. 1 tablespoon chopped parsley
¼ cup coarse bread crumbs, or matzo meal
1 onion, finely chopped. Pepper. Nutmeg
⅓ cup (50 g. or 2 oz.) chopped almonds. 4 egg yolks
2 to 3 tablespoons (6 to 9 g.) cornstarch

Scale and clean fish; rinse well. Remove fish meat and bones, taking care not to damage the skin, head and tail. Put the raw fish through a meat grinder. Cover fish bones in a kettle with water seasoned with salt, lemon juice and soup greens; cook 25 minutes. Strain; reserve broth.
Heat butter in a skillet; add fish, parsley and crumbs and cook several minutes. Mix in the onion, pepper, nutmeg, almonds and 2 egg yolks mixed with a little *water*. Stuff mixture into fish skin; close fish with skewers, or sew with thread. Lay fish gently into heated broth and simmer until done; remove to heated platter and keep warm while preparing the sauce.
Thicken broth in kettle with cornstarch mixed with a little cold *water*. Stir the remaining 2 egg yolks into the sauce. Add seasoning, if needed. Pour sauce over fish on platter and garnish with *lemon slices.*
4 servings
Note: If desired, omit cornstarch and reduce the strained broth to sauce consistency.

34

Chicken Salad with Celery
United States

The Americans have invented many attractive salads combining meat or poultry with chopped vegetables and appropriate fruits. There are epicurean puritans who reject such cooking practices as highly objectionable; nevertheless, Americans are not alone in their liking for these unusual salad combinations. Connoisseurs in many other countries seem to enjoy them also. Americans use chicken in a wide variety of salad combinations. Here, for example, is a refreshing salad using leftover cooked chicken with fruits and vegetables.

1¾ cups (250 g. or 9 oz.) cubed cooked chicken
1 cup (100 g. or 3½ oz.) diagonally sliced celery;
or use cooked celery root (celeriac), cut in sticks
1 small onion, minced. Juice of 1 lemon. Salt
½ cup (75 g. or 2½ oz.) slivered almonds, toasted
12 pimento-stuffed olives, sliced
1 cup (100 g. or 3½ oz.) grapes, halved,
and seeds removed
1 small can mandarin oranges, drained
Mayonnaise

Combine chicken, celery and onion in a bowl; sprinkle lemon juice over mixture, season to taste and toss gently to mix ingredients. Chill in refrigerator about 1 hour.

When ready to serve, add almonds, olives, grapes and mandarin oranges. Gently toss with enough mayonnaise to moisten ingredients. Serve salad on crisp *greens*.

4 servings

Note: If desired, substitute cooked turkey for chicken, toasted pecans for almonds and thick sour cream or whipped cream for some of the mayonnaise.

35

Veal Scallops
Switzerland

The meat specialty from Zurich, made of boneless slices of veal flattened and cut into small pieces (scallops), has won many friends outside of Switzerland. One of many well known Swiss veal preparations, Veal Scallops, is an easy and quickly prepared dish with flavors to satisfy discriminating epicurean tastes.

1 lb. (500 g.) boneless veal (cutlet or steak)
4 tablespoons butter or margarine
1 onion, finely chopped. Flour
½ cup (⅛ liter or about ¼ pt.) white wine
½ cup (⅛ liter or about ¼ pt.) broth or bouillon
Salt. Pepper. 1 tablespoon chopped parsley

Put the veal on a cutting board. Pound with a meat hammer until very thin. Cut the meat into small pieces (scallops).
Melt the butter in a heatproof casserole or skillet. Add chopped onion to skillet; cook several minutes, stirring occasionally, or until lightly browned.
Dredge meat pieces with flour and put into casserole. Cook quickly over high heat until the veal is lightly browned. Stir in wine, broth, salt and pepper. Cook several minutes longer, stirring occasionally. Remove from heat; let stand a few minutes, then sprinkle with chopped parsley.
Serve with noodles, sliced tomatoes and lettuce salad or other vegetable salad, or (as customary in Zurich) with applesauce.
4 servings

Note: If desired, stir a small amount of cream and some sautéed chopped mushrooms into the sauce.

Green Sauce
Italy, Germany

On an Italian menu, the sauce is known as Salsa Verde. In Frankfurt, Germany, it is called Grie Soss. It can be prepared using mayonnaise or a blend of vinegar and salad oil as a base. According to tradition, Green Sauce should contain at least seven herbs that are chopped as finely as possible. As it is served in most Italian restaurants today, however, Salsa Verde derives its green color only from fresh spinach.

In Goethe's time in Frankfurt, the chopped herbs were marinated in vinegar and oil. Mashed egg yolks, spices and sour cream were then added and the ingredients were forced through a sieve. If the sauce still was not green enough, spinach juice was blended into achieve the desired color.

This versatile sauce goes well with cold cooked fish and meat, especially beef or corned beef and with chilled cooked vegetables such as asparagus, green beans, broccoli, or potatoes, or with a salad of tomatoes, cucumbers, eggs, artichoke hearts, olives and radishes.

Suggestion 1:

⅔ cup (125 g.) mayonnaise (use half yogurt, if desired)
Salt. Pepper
6 tablespoons chopped herbs (parsley, dill, chives, chervil, sorrel, watercress, borage, tarragon)
2 hard-cooked eggs, chopped

Suggestion 2:

½ cup (⅛ liter or about ¼ pt.) each salad oil and vinegar
1 cup finely chopped parsley
Salt. Pepper. Sugar to taste
1 to 2 tablespoons chopped capers

For each suggestion, combine all ingredients in the order given. Chill at least 30 minutes before serving.
Note: See Bollito Misto recipe for another version of Salsa Verde.

Gulyáshus
Hungary

In Hungarian, gulyas means herdsman or shepherd. The herdsman's favorite meat dish, called Gulyáshus is said to have originated back in the ninth century. Tradition has it that the shepherds cooked cubes of meat with onion in a heavy kettle, with little moisture added. (No paprika was used, since the pepper pod from South America had not yet been introduced to the Europeans.) When all the liquid had evaporated, the pieces of meat were dried in the sun and then stored in a bag made of the sheep's stomach. The shepherds added water before reheating the meat for future servings.

Nowadays, Gulyáshus and paprika are inseparable. No flour should be used for thickening, and no spice except caraway is used; but, within these limits, many variations are possible. You may use fresh tomatoes or tomato purée, garlic, sliced green peppers or hot cherry peppers to make the dish very spicy.

8 tablespoons (100 g. or 4 oz.) lard or other fat
1 lb. (500 g.) onions, sliced
1 large garlic clove, crushed
3 to 4 tablespoons tomato paste
2 lbs. (1 kg.) boneless lean beef, cut in pieces
1 tablespoon paprika
⅛ to ¼ teaspoon caraway seed. Salt to taste
4 tablespoons thick sour cream

Heat lard in a heatproof casserole or skillet. Add onion and garlic; cook about 5 minutes, stirring occasionally. Add tomato paste and beef; stir until thoroughly mixed. Sprinkle with paprika and add a small amount of *water* or *broth.* Cover casserole tightly and cook over low heat until meat is tender; if necessary, add more liquid during cooking. Add caraway seed and salt. Blend in sour cream; season with paprika and salt to taste. Serve hot with potatoes, bread, dumplings or noodles.
About 6 servings

Mutton Pilaf
Turkey

Pilaf, also spelled Pilav, Pilaw or Pilaff, is a dish originating in the Middle East and consisting mostly of rice. In that part of the world, as well as in North Africa, Pilaf is served as often as potatoes are in other countries. "There are as many Pilafs as minarets", says a Turkish proverb. Besides being used as an accompaniment for meat dishes, Pilaf also appears in the Middle Eastern cuisine as a main dish with meat or poultry and vegetables, all combined with the well seasoned rice. The best known is Mutton Pilaf which, in its original form, was seasoned only with salt and saffron. The following recipe is somewhat Europeanized. Should you desire a more oriental preparation, omit tomato paste and paprika and season only with a pinch of saffron diluted in a little rose water.

3 tablespoons olive oil. 1 garlic clove
3 tablespoons blanched almonds. 2 onions, chopped
1 lb. (500 g.) mutton, cut in pieces
Salt. Paprika. 2 tablespoons tomato paste
3 cups (¾ liter or about 1½ pts.) broth or bouillon
1⅓ cups (250 g. or 10 oz.) long-grain rice
⅔ cup (100 g. or 3½ oz.) raisins

Heat oil in heatproof casserole or skillet. Add garlic and almonds; heat until almonds are lightly browned. Remove garlic and almonds; set almonds aside and discard garlic. Add chopped onion to skillet and cook 2 minutes; add meat and brown on all sides. Season with salt and paprika. Stir tomato paste into broth and add to the meat. Cover and cook gently 1 hour, or until meat is almost tender. Mix in rice and raisins. Cook covered, over low heat about 20 minutes, or until rice is soft. Sprinkle almonds over Pilaf and serve with lettuce and tomato salad.
About 6 servings

Chicken Marengo
France

Napoleon's cook, Dunant, a native of Switzerland, improvised this famous dish after the Battle of Marengo of June 14, 1800. After having beaten the Austrians, the First Consul demanded food. Unfortunately, Dunant had lost his entire rations. So he ordered some soldiers to go out and find something edible. One brought back a chicken another tomatoes, a third some eggs and a fourth two crabs. And that, according to legend, is how Chicken Marengo was born.

4 tablespoons oil
1 boiler-fryer chicken, cut in serving pieces
Salt, pepper. 1 garlic clove, crushed
2 onions, chopped. 1 tablespoon flour
2 medium tomatoes, cut in pieces. 1 glass white wine
½ cup (⅛ liter or about ¼ pt.) broth or bouillon
½ bay leaf. 1 whole clove. 4 peppercorns
2 to 3 teaspoons (6 to 9 g.) cornstarch
Mushroom caps, browned in butter
2 eggs. Butter
2 boiled crabs, or 1 can (5 oz. or 150 g.) crab meat
White bread

Heat oil in heatproof casserole or skillet; add chicken and sprinkle with salt and pepper. Brown pieces evenly on all sides over medium heat; remove from casserole.
Fry garlic and onion in hot oil; stir in flour and tomatoes. Mix well and blend in wine and broth. Add bay leaf, clove, and peppercorns; cook and stir until boiling. Return chicken to casserole, cover and cook slowly until tender. Remove chicken and keep warm.
Strain the sauce into a saucepan; thicken with cornstarch blended with a little *cold water*. Season to taste.
Heat mushrooms in the sauce. Fry eggs in a small amount of butter. Heat crab meat in butter. Serve chicken with sauce, toasted bread slices, eggs and crab meat on a preheated platter.
4 servings

40

Chicken Curry
India

English colonial officers derived "curry" from the Tamil word "kari." In cooking, curry has two meanings. It may refer to curry powder, a mixture of spices that homemakers use in dishes. In India, the spices are freshly ground with a stone mortar and pestle, the homemaker choosing the appropriate blend for each occasion. The second meaning is that any dish traditionally from India that is seasoned primarily with curry powder is considered a curry. Such dishes as chicken curry and fish curry are examples. Indian cooks maintain that European curry dishes are only faintly reminiscent of the true Indian curries. But how many occasions does one have to go to India for sample tasting?

1 stewing chicken
Soup greens (see note with Bollito Misto)
1 teaspoon salt
4 tablespoons (50 g. or 2 oz.) butter or margarine
7 tablespoons (50 g. or 2 oz.) flour
2 to 3 teaspoons curry powder
½ to 1 teaspoon salt. Juice of 1 lemon
½ cup (115 g. or ¼ pt.) thick sour cream
4 slices pineapple, quartered (or use 1 can pineapple chunks, drained)

Cook chicken with soup greens in just enough *boiling salted water* to cover. When chicken is tender, remove from the broth and cut into serving-sized pieces. Strain the chicken broth.

Heat butter in heatproof casserole or saucepot over medium heat; blend in the flour. Lower heat and cook, stirring constantly, until flour is browned. Gradually add 2 cups (½ liter) of the chicken broth. Cook and stir until thickened and smooth; cook slowly about 5 minutes longer. Season with curry powder, salt and lemon juice. Blend in sour cream. Add pineapple slices and chicken and heat through. Garnish with sweet red pepper strips. Serve with fluffy rice.

4 servings

Note: If desired, add ¼ teaspoon pepper or ½ teaspoon paprika to curry.

Lobster Armoricaine
France

The origin of this gourmet specialty has been a controversial issue for many years, French and American chefs both claiming it. To further confuse the issue, the dish appears on some menus as Lobster (Homard) Americaine which in French means "in the American manner", and on others as Lobster (Homard) Amoricaine meaning "in the manner of Brittany", that part of France that was once called by the Roman name "Amorica".

Some culinary researchers do not believe it originated in Brittany, since the dish uses tomatoes, garlic, herbs and oil, which indicate it is more characteristic of Provence. Other researchers have concluded that the use of the word Americaine refers to America and the American patrons who first enjoyed it in a certain Paris restaurant. Whatever the origin, it is a truly deluxe dish.

2 live lobsters. Salt
1½ cups (⅛ liter or about ¼ pt.) olive oil
3 oz. (100 g.) shallots, chopped
1 garlic clove, crushed. 1 carrot, chopped
½ teaspoon each thyme and tarragon
Cayenne pepper. 1 glass brandy
1 small can tomato sauce
½ cup (⅛ liter or about ¼ pt.) dry white wine

Remove and crack open the claws from lobsters. Remove tail sections from lobsters and divide into 3 or 4 slices. Halve the lobsters lengthwise and discard veins and sacs. Remove livers and corals and set aside. Rub in salt on all places where lobster was cut open.

Heat oil in a heavy skillet; add shallot, garlic, carrot, thyme and tarragon. Cook and stir about 2 minutes. Add lobster and sprinkle with a little cayenne pepper. Pour in brandy, ignite and let stand until flame subsides. Add tomato sauce, cover and simmer until shells are red and lobster meat is tender.

Cool slightly and remove lobster meat from shells. Strain the sauce and add livers and corals. Cook, stirring constantly several minutes or until thickened. Add the white wine. Add lobster meat and reheat to serving temperature.

4 servings

42

Lobster Cocktail
United States

Although lobster is not exactly a reasonably priced delicacy, it can be served occasionally for a special occasion meal. Other shellfish such as crab meat or shrimp may also be used with the sauce described here. Live lobster mainly comes from Scandinavia, the United States and Canada. Although this particular cocktail is an American creation, similar preparations are to be found in other countries where lobster is a much appreciated delicacy.

Suggestion 1:

7 oz. (200 g.) fresh or canned lobster meat
1 small can asparagus spears, drained
1 small can mushrooms, drained
⅔ cup (125 g. or about ¼ pt.) mayonnaise
2 tablespoons tomato paste
3 tablespoons evaporated milk or yogurt
Salt. Pepper. Lemon juice. Brandy
Sugar. Parsley

Suggestion 2:

11 oz. (300 g.) canned lobster meat
1 tablespoon brandy. 1 tablespoon dry sherry
1 tablespoon tomato ketchup. 2 tablespoons mayonnaise
3 tablespoons cream. 1 tablespoon lemon juice
1 tablespoon finely chopped gherkins

1. Separate lobster meat into equal chunks; cut asparagus and mushrooms as desired. Blend remaining ingredients. Arrange lobster meat in cocktail glasses or bowls. Cover with sauce and chill about 1 hour. Serve with toast.
2. Combine all ingredients except lobster, mixing well. Serve over lobster meat as in 1.
4 servings

Hutspot
Netherlands

This hearty, nutritious dish is a Dutch favorite. However, several other countries have similar dishes—for example, the French and Belgian Hochepot and the English Hotpot. Usually potatoes are used in all versions, along with other vegetables and meat. The Dutch make the dish with beef; the Scots use mutton, sometimes with beef added; and the French and Belgians include pigs' ears and feet along with other meat.

11 oz. (300 g.) dried navy (pea) beans
1 lb. (500 g.) fresh brisket of beef. 1 bay leaf
Soup greens (see note with Bollito Misto). Salt
1 lb. (500 g.) carrots. 6 medium potatoes
3 onions, chopped. 8 tablespoons (100 g. or 4 oz.) butter
or margarine, browned
Parsley sprigs

Put beans into a large saucepan and pour in *water* to cover. Cover saucepan and allow beans to soak overnight. Or, bring beans and water to boiling; boil 2 minutes. Remove saucepan from heat. Cover; set beans aside to soak 1 hour.

When beans have soaked, put meat, bay leaf and soup greens into a saucepot with *lightly salted water*. Cover and cook about 2 hours. Meanwhile, bring the beans with soaking water to boiling; cover and cook about 1 hour.

Clean, pare and dice carrots and potatoes. Add carrot, potato, onion and partially cooked beans to meat; cook until meat and vegetables are tender. Remove meat and slice. Discard bay leaf. Mash vegetables and spoon into a large shallow serving dish. Pour browned butter over vegetables. Overlap meat slices along the center and garnish with parsley. *About 6 servings*

Imam Bayildi
Turkey

This stuffed eggplant dish, along with Pilaf and Shashlik, is one of Turkey's great national specialties.

An Imam is an Islamic leader. Imam Bayildi literally translated, means "the Imam collapsed". Whether he did it out of enthusiasm for this tasty preparation or because he had overeaten is not known exactly. In any case, the name of this dish suggests a culinary delight. Here is our version of the recipe.

4 medium eggplants. Salt. Pepper.
½ cup (⅛ liter or about ¼ pt.) olive oil
2 onions, coarsely chopped. 4 small tomatoes, sliced
1 garlic clove, crushed. Chopped parsley
½ to 1 teaspoon sugar. 1 bay leaf
1 tablespoon finely chopped almonds

Cut the eggplants into halves lengthwise; score the surface crosswise, leaving shell intact. Sprinkle with salt and pepper. Sauté the eggplant halves in hot oil in a skillet until the meat can be scooped out easily with a spoon. Remove from skillet. Add onion, two thirds of the sliced tomatoes, garlic, chopped parsley and scooped-out eggplant pieces to oil in skillet and cook several minutes. Season with salt, pepper, sugar and bay leaf (to be removed later). Finally, stir in the chopped almonds. Stuff eggplant shells with this mixture.

Arrange in a well greased ovenproof dish, cover with the remaining tomato slices and sprinkle lightly with salt and pepper.

Bake in a moderately hot oven (375-400°F or 190-200°C) about 15 minutes. Serve hot or cold.

4 servings

Irish Stew
Ireland

The famous Irish Stew made with mutton is one of those national specialties that is prepared in many different ways in its own country. Furthermore, it has been varied in foreign countries to such an extent that in many instances it only remotely resembles an Irish recipe.

All Irish Stews seem to have three ingredients in common: mutton, potatoes and onions. Cabbage and carrots are often included also. On the continent, white turnips, celery and leeks are added, although the Irish disapprove of these ingredients. Cloves are also used occasionally. The following suggestion comes from a Dublin restaurant.

1¾ lbs. (750 g.) mutton (shoulder, shank, or neck)
4 onions. 2 carrots. 1¾ lbs. (750 g.) cabbage
1 lb. (500 g.) potatoes. 1¾ lbs. (750 g.) thinly sliced bacon
Salt. Pepper. 1 bay leaf. 2 teaspoons cumin seed

Trim fat from the mutton and cut meat into pieces. Put into a saucepot and add just enough water to cover meat. Cook, covered, 1½ hours.

Meanwhile, cut onions into quarters; cut carrots and cabbage into strips and quarter the potatoes. Cover the bottom of a large heatproof casserole with slices of bacon. Cover with alternate layers of mutton, onion, carrot, cabbage and potato; season layers with remaining ingredients. Pour over all enough *mutton stock* (broth) to barely cover the top layer. Bring to boiling; cover tightly and simmer 20 to 30 minutes, or until meat and vegetables are tender. Sprinkle with chopped parsley, if desired.

About 4 servings

Kaiserschmarrn
Austria

In Austria, southern Germany and Bohemia, a Kaiserschmarrn is a unique dessert dish made from pancakes torn into large pieces and tossed with sugar and raisins. Melted butter and cinnamon are sometimes added.

Many legends surround this dessert's creation. One of them is that Emperor Franz Joseph, while hunting in the forest one day, lost his way. A farmer's wife took pity on him, offering him an unsuccessfully baked pancake, and thus kept him from starving.

According to another story, the dish was created in honor of Empress Elizabeth ("Sissy"), who usually disliked dishes prepared with flour. So the dessert was called Kaiserschmarrn (or "the emperor's omelet"), so that the ingredients would be disguised. Or it may be possible that the name is a normal etymological variation of Kaserschmarrn, (Kaser-Senn) a word that originally meant cheesemaker. Somewhere along the line, the dessert became popular with the nobility and thus became Kaiserschmarrn.

5 eggs, separated. ½ teaspoon salt
½ cup (100 g. or 3½ oz.) sugar
2 cups (about 240 g. or 8 oz.) flour
½ cup (⅛ liter or about ¼ pt.) milk
4 tablespoons butter, melted
Grated peel of ½ lemon. Shortening for frying
½ cup (100 g. or 3½ oz.) raisins, scalded
and dried on absorbent paper
Sugar

Beat egg yolks with salt and sugar until very thick; add flour alternately with milk, beating until smooth after each addition. Beat in melted butter and grated peel. Beat egg whites until stiff peaks are formed; fold into the batter.

Heat enough shortening to coat the bottom of skillet; pour on enough batter to cover bottom, tipping skillet back and forth to cover evenly. Bake over medium heat until pancake is lightly browned on both sides. Then tear into pieces with two forks. Sprinkle with some of the raisins and sugar, tossing gently while heating to golden brown.

Repeat process until all the batter is used. Serve pancakes immediately with apple sauce or fruit compôte.
6 servings

47

Veal Steak Cordon Bleu
Switzerland

This cheese-ham schnitzel is so famous that several countries claim the honor of having prepared it first. Presumably, it was first introduced as "Swiss cheese Schnitzel". It might have received its present name in a cooking contest.

"Cordon Bleu" means "blue ribbon". Once upon a time, the Cordon Bleu belonged to the French Order of Knights of the Holy Spirit and was presented only to brave men. However, Louis XV of France also awarded it to the cook of his mistress, the beautiful and notorious Countess DuBarry. Ever since then, the term Cordon Bleu has been applied not only to a cook who has learned his culinary art as well as has the chef de cuisine, but also to an especially successful meal.

**8 veal steaks or cutlets. Salt. Pepper
Tomato ketchup. 4 slices cooked ham
4 slices Swiss cheese. Flour. 1 egg. Bread crumbs
Shortening. 1 lemon**

Flatten steaks by pounding them lightly with a meat hammer. Season with salt and pepper. Spread a thin layer of ketchup over one side of each steak. Fold a very thin slice of cooked ham over a slice of cheese and put it between two veal steaks (ketchup side faces inside). Secure with wooden picks.

Dip steaks in flour, then in lightly beaten egg; coat with bread crumbs. Fry in hot shortening in a heavy skillet until evenly browned on both sides. (Cook slowly so that veal will be tender when it has browned sufficiently.) Serve with lemon wedges, buttered cauliflower and a tossed salad.
4 servings

Note: If thicker veal steaks are used, cut a pocket lengthwise into steak and carefully insert ham and cheese.

Polish Carp
Poland

This fish dish, also known as Carp à la Polonaise, has several different versions. In each version, the blood of the carp is used to make a sauce in which the whole carp or pieces of it are cooked. Polish carp is considered a Christmas dinner specialty in Silesia. Before World War II, Silesia supplied fifty percent of Germany's carp.

The sauce served with the fish is prepared in various ways, with such ingredients as raisins and almonds, the carp's roe, and honey or syrup used in its preparation.

1 live carp. Vinegar
2 cups (½ liter or ¾ pt.) beer
6 small onions, sliced. Salt. 6 peppercorns
1 bay leaf. Lemon juice. 1 teaspoon sugar
2 tablespoons butter
¾ cup (75 g. or 3 oz.) gingersnap crumbs
(about 10 gingersnaps)

Reserve blood from a freshly killed carp; mix it with a little vinegar and set aside.

Clean and remove inside of carp, taking care not to damage the gall; wash thoroughly. Cut fish into four pieces.

In a saucepan, mix beer with *2 cups (½ liter or about 1 pint) water*. Add onion, salt, peppercorns, bay leaf, lemon juice, sugar and butter. Cook 20 minutes, stirring occasionally. Strain liquid, return to saucepan and add carp blood; beat to blend well. Stir in gingersnap crumbs. Bring to boiling. Put pieces of carp into sauce and cook over low heat about 30 minutes.

Arrange pieces of carp on a preheated platter. Strain sauce again; season to taste and pour some of it over carp. Serve remaining sauce separately in a sauceboat. If desired, accompany with sauerkraut.

4 servings

49

Kedgeree
India

Kedgeree is a spicy mixture of beans (or peas), rice and onions, a much appreciated East Indian dish. Similar versions of the dish have such names as Kaderi, Khideri, Khicharke and Kitscher. In England it is known as Kedgeree, also Kegeree, and is usually served for breakfast or lunch. Most English versions include flaked fish such as finnan haddie and salt cod, along with hard-cooked eggs and spices.

13 oz. (375 g.) dried split peas. 5 tablespoons oil
2 large onions, sliced. 13 oz. (375 g.) long grain rice
5 peppercorns. 1 bay leaf. 1 teaspoon curry powder
¼ teaspoon ginger. ⅛ teaspoon mace, optional
Salt to taste. 3 hard-cooked eggs, cut in halves

Cover dried peas with cold *water* in a saucepot and soak for 2 hours; drain well.

Heat oil in a heatproof casserole or saucepot; add onion and cook until lightly browned. Add rice and split peas, stirring well; add enough boiling *water* to fill pot 2 inches (5 centimeters) above the mixture. Bring to boiling and add a mixture of the spices and salt. Cover and cook over medium heat 35 to 40 minutes or until rice and peas are tender. Garnish with hard-cooked eggs and, if desired, additional fried onion rings.
About 6 servings

Kedgeree with Fish: Cook ½ *cup chopped onion* in *3 tablespoons butter* or *margarine* about 2 minutes in a heavy saucepan. Add 2 cups *each flaked cooked fish* and *fluffy cooked rice*. Combine ½ *cup cream* with ½ *teaspoon curry powder*. Add to saucepan. Season to taste with *salt* and *pepper*. Cook and stir until mixture is very hot. Add 3 *hard-cooked eggs, chopped* and 3 *tablespoons chopped parsley*. Heat several minutes longer and serve.
4 or 5 servings

Kuskus
North Africa

The native dish of the Arabs and Berbers is not easy to prepare, but you will be rewarded with a hearty, very savory dish. In North Africa, the cooked semolina is molded with the right hand (the left hand is considered impure) into balls, which are then pushed into one's own mouth or that of the honored guest. Semolina is the grainlike part of the wheat remaining in the sieve after the fine flour has been sifted through. The word kuskus seems to come from the Arabic word keskes, or a semolina sieve.

1 lb. (500 g.) lean mutton, cut in pieces
8 tablespoons (100 g. or 4 oz.) butter or margarine
1 onion, chopped. 1 clove garlic, crushed
Salt. Pepper. 1 bay leaf. 1 kohlrabi, pared
2 tomatoes. 2 green peppers. 3 carrots
½ cup green peas. 1 tablespoon tomato paste
1 teaspoon Tabasco. ½ lb. (250 g.) coarse semolina

Brown mutton in a saucepot in half the butter; add chopped onion and crushed garlic; cook 3 minutes. Season with salt and pepper; add bay leaf and just enough *water* to cover meat. Cover and cook for about 45 minutes over medium heat.
Slice or cut into strips kohlrabi, tomatoes, green peppers and carrots; add to meat along with the peas. Stir in tomato paste and Tabasco.
Wet semolina with approximately ½ cup *(⅛ liter or scant ¼ pint) hot salted water* and form ricelike crumbs with your hands. Put semolina crumbs in a sieve that fits or can be hung over the mixture in pot. (Make sure the semolina does not touch the liquid in pot.) Cover saucepot. If cover does not fit tightly because of the sieve, place a clean cloth between cover and saucepot. Continue cooking for about 1 hour or until meat and vegetables are tender. Season meat to taste and toss the steamed semolina with *melted butter.* Serve in separate dishes.
About 6 servings

Lucca-Augen (Lucca-Eyes)
Germany

Pauline Lucca, born in Vienna in 1842, was a celebrated opera singer at the Royal Court Opera in Berlin, where she studied under Giacomo Meyerbeer. She had triumphant successes at the world's greatest opera houses in Vienna, London, Petersburg and in America. "Mrs. Lucca's successes," a contemporary critic wrote, "are not so much due to her voice or her technique, but rather to the fascinating charm of her appearance which makes her performances unforgettable". She was a beautiful woman, who not only had "a golden throat" but must also have had eyes of shining brightness. Why else would the chef de cuisine of the Berlin restaurant Kempinski have created Lucca-Eyes, a delicacy of raw beef, caviar and oysters? Another Berlin specialty, a kind of frosted éclair filled with vanilla cream or sweetened whipped cream, was also given the same name.

4 slices white bread, crusts removed
½ lb. (250 g.) lean boneless beef, finely ground
2 egg yolks, slightly beaten. ½ medium onion, grated
Salt. Pepper. Worcestershire sauce
1 small can caviar. 4 fresh oysters

Toast the slices of bread. Mix ground beef thoroughly with the egg yolks. Season with onion, salt, pepper and Worcestershire sauce. Spread the mixture ⅜ inch (1 centimeter) thick on each toast square. Top each square with caviar and a raw oyster so that it gives the appearance of an eye with an eyebrow. Serve on a bed of crisp *greens* as an hors d'oeuvre for a festive or special occasion breakfast or lunch.
4 servings

Minestrone
Italy

Derived from the Latin "to hand out", this Italian soup was a staple diet in the days when the monks kept it always on the fire to be ready for sojourners or travelers. A spicy vegetable soup that contains macaroni or some other pasta, or rice, it is hearty enough to be served as a main course for lunch. Here is an especially flavorful and appetite-satisfying version of the soup using both meat and vegetables.

> 1 lb. (500 g.) beef soup meat. 5 peppercorns
> Soup greens (see note with Bollito Misto). Salt
> ¼ lb. (125 g.) lean smoked bacon, diced
> 2 tablespoons oil. 1 onion, chopped
> 2 garlic cloves, chopped. 2 large tomatoes, peeled
> 2 carrots, sliced or diced. 2 leeks, chopped
> 2 kohlrabi, pared and diced. 2 potatoes, pared and diced
> ½ lb. (250 g.) green beans, cut in pieces
> ½ lb. (250 g.) green peas
> ½ can white (navy) beans, drained
> ¼ lb. (125 g.) spaghetti
> Salt. Pepper. Basil, majoram, and thyme
> Shredded Parmesan cheese

Combine beef, peppercorns and soup greens in a soup kettle containing lightly salted *water*. Bring to boiling and cook, covered, 2 to 3 hours. Strain broth and dice the meat. Return broth and meat to kettle.

Lightly brown the bacon in oil in a skillet over medium heat. Add chopped onion and garlic. Cook until golden. Add tomatoes and cook in skillet about 3 minutes. Add to soup mixture in kettle and bring to boiling. Add diced or sliced carrots, leeks, kohlrabi, potatoes, green beans and peas. Cook until vegetables are half done. Add white beans and spaghetti. Cook until spaghetti is tender.

Season soup with salt, pepper and herbs. Serve in a soup tureen. Accompany with the Parmesan cheese.

4 servings

Mock Turtle Soup
England

A genuine turtle soup is an epicurean delicacy, a specialty not everybody can afford. Therefore, the English, "who, as everyone knows, would do anything for turtle soup," says the famous culinary reference book, *Larousse Gastronomique,* created a substitute and called it Mock Turtle Soup. This substitute became known as a gourmet specialty in many countries. The preparation is somewhat complicated and time consuming but is well worth the effort. Here is the original English recipe.

1 calf's head. Salt
Soup greens (see note with Bollito Misto)
4 tablespoons butter or margarine
½ cup (80 g. or 3 oz.) julienne ham strips
1 onion, chopped. 1 carrot, chopped
2 stalks celery, diagonally sliced. 4 tablespoons flour
1 glass sherry. 1 tablespoon lemon juice. Salt. Pepper
1 small can mushrooms, drained and cut in halves

Clean calf's head and put into a saucepot with soup greens and lightly salted *water.* Bring to boiling and simmer until the meat can be easily removed from the bone. Set aside. Remove the calf's head and strain the broth.

Heat butter in skillet; add ham, chopped onion, carrot and celery. Blend in flour and the broth. Cook and stir until mixture comes to boiling. Lower heat and cook about 10 minutes, stirring occasionally. Stir in wine and lemon juice. Season to taste with salt and pepper. Remove the meat from calf's head and cut into strips; add with the mushroom halves to soup mixture. Cook over low heat about 5 minutes, or until of serving temperature. Ladle into soup bowls.
4 servings

Note: If desired, substitute for the calf's head 1 pound (500 g.) veal bones with some meat on the bones.

Mulligatawny Soup
India, England

This Indian soup, the name of which means "pepper water", originated as a simple broth seasoned with a sharp curry mixture. However, the English living in India preferred a more hearty soup, so they added mutton and vegetables to the well seasoned broth.

Since mutton is not always appreciated by everyone, a version substituting chicken for the mutton was developed. The chicken adaptation has found favor on the European continent and even Australia. Today Mulligatawny sometimes appears on menus as a thin clear soup and sometimes as a very thick stewlike dish flavored with curry and made with meat, or more often with chicken. A variety of other ingredients such as rice, apple, egg and lemon juice, are usually added.

1 stewing or frying chicken, cut in pieces
1 to 1½ teaspoons salt. 1 onion
Soup greens (see note with Bollito Misto)
1 bay leaf
5 slices (75 g. or 2½ oz.) lean smoked bacon
3 tablespoons butter. 4 tomatoes, peeled and chopped
5 tablespoons flour. 2 to 3 teaspoons curry powder
Cayenne pepper. ½ cup (⅛ liter or about ¼ pt.) cream

Place chicken, salt, onion, soup greens and bay leaf in a saucepot or kettle; add water to cover. Cook over medium heat until chicken is tender. Remove meat from bones and cut into strips. Strain the broth. Dice bacon and sauté about 3 minutes in hot butter in a saucepan. Add chopped tomato and cook 2 minutes longer. Blend in flour and mix well. Stir in the chicken broth and cook 15 minutes, stirring occasionally. Season with curry powder and cayenne pepper. Add cream and serve with toasted white bread cubes or fluffy rice.

About 6 servings

Musaka
Orient

This mixture of ground meat and vegetables originated in Turkey but can be found today throughout the countries once dominated by Turks—especially Yugoslavia, Greece and Bulgaria. Generally lamb or mutton is used. The following recipe uses a mixture of ground beef and pork along with eggplant. Potatoes are optional. Important is the custard-like sauce, the so-called Saliwka.

3 medium potatoes. Salt
½ cup (⅛ liter or about ¼ pt.) oil
4 small eggplants. 2 onions, finely chopped
1 lb. (500 g.) beef and pork, ground. Pepper. Paprika
Thyme, rosemary, sage. 2 tablespoons tomato purée
½ cup (⅛ liter or about ¼ pt.) broth or bouillon
Sauce (Saliwka):
1 cup (230 g. or about ½ pt.) yogurt
3 eggs. ⅛ teaspoon baking powder
2 tablespoons flour. Salt

Pare and slice (or dice) potatoes; salt lightly and brown in heated oil in a large heavy skillet and set aside.

Pare and slice eggplants lengthwise; sprinkle with *salt,* and set aside for 30 minutes. Fry them in 3 or 4 tablespoons of the hot oil till eggplant meat is tender.

Heat a little oil in a skillet; add onions and ground meat and cook about 5 minutes. Add eggplant; season to taste and let simmer for a few minutes, stirring occasionally.

Add tomato purée and broth; bring to boiling.

Arrange alternative layers of potatoes and the ground meat mixture in a greased baking dish. Cover and set in a moderate oven (350°F or 180°C) for 40 minutes.

Mix yogurt with other ingredients. Pour over the Musaka, cover and return to oven for another 10 minutes. Place under broiler heat a few minutes to brown well on top. Serve immediately.

About 6 servings

Nasi Goreng
Indonesia

The words Nasi Goreng mean "fried rice". It refers to an Indonesian main dish that consists of a mixture of rice, chicken and shrimp and is sometimes served with numerous side dishes. The Dutch have made it popular in Europe and it is now well known in America.

No two Nasi Goreng dishes are ever prepared in the same way, but it is safe to say that anyone who lives in Indonesia or Malaysia has enjoyed some version of this spicy dish. It has pronounced Chinese overtones in its method of preparation and exotic flavors and the dish might have originated in China. However, the Chinese begin its preparation by using boiled rice. The Indonesians usually sauté the rice in a generous amount of oil before cooking it in liquid.

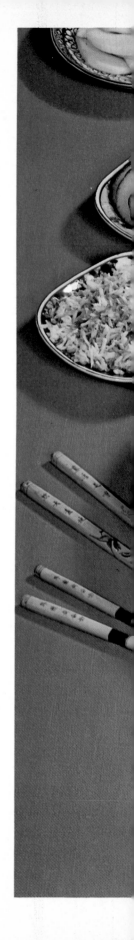

6 tablespoons oil. 1 onion, chopped
1 large garlic clove, crushed. 1 tablespoon curry powder
Salt. Sugar. ¾ lb. (350 g.) cooked chicken
2 tomatoes, peeled and sliced
3 cups (600 g. or 1½ lbs.) cooked rice
1 cup cooked shrimp
1 tablespoon lemon juice. Onion rings

Heat oil in a skillet; add onion and garlic and sauté about 3 minutes, stirring gently. Blend in the curry; add salt and sugar to taste. Cut the chicken into julienne strips; peel and slice tomatoes; add chicken and tomatoes to skillet and continue sautéeing several minutes. Mix in the cooked rice and the shrimp. Heat mixture to serving temperature and turn into a serving dish. Sprinkle with lemon juice and garnish with fried onion rings.

Accompany Nasi Goreng with a variety of side dishes: tomato salad, bits of pineapple, shredded coconut, salted peanuts, marinated cucumber slices, fried banana slices, chopped hard-cooked eggs, apple slices, tomato ketchup, chili sauce, soy sauce, mango and peach chutney and candied ginger.

4 servings

Olla Podrida
Spain, South America

For the Spaniards and most South Americans, Olla Podrida, the Spanish casserole dish, comes immediately after God, if one is to believe a well known Spanish proverb. Also called Puchero or Cocido, this Spanish national dish consists of several kinds of meat and vegetables. It has many variations, depending upon taste and ingredients available. The authentic Spanish version lists Spanish sausages (chorizos) and chick peas (garbanzos) among its ingredients.

½ lb. (250 g.) dried yellow peas. 2 tablespoons oil
2 onions, chopped. 1 garlic clove, crushed
½ lb. (250 g.) beef. ½ lb. (250 g.) mutton
½ lb. (250 g.) ham
1¾ lbs. (750 g.) chicken, cut up
3 small garlic sausages (chorizos), sliced
Salt. Pepper. Cumin seed, chervil
¼ head white cabbage, sliced
1 celery root (celeriac), sliced
½ lb. (250 g.) carrots, sliced
½ lb. (250 g.) green beans, cut
1 head lettuce, cut in quarters

Soak peas overnight in water to cover. The next day, drain the peas and put into a saucepot with *2 quarts (2 liters) water*. Bring to boiling and cook 30 minutes.
Heat oil in a large skillet or saucepot. Add chopped onion and crushed garlic; cook 3 minutes, stirring occasionally. Cut beef, mutton and ham into large pieces. Add to the skillet with the chicken. Cook until meat is browned. Add the sliced chorizo and the peas with cooking water. Season and cook over medium heat 1½ to 2 hours. Add cabbage, celery root, carrots, green beans and lettuce. Cook over medium heat until vegetables are tender. Turn into a serving dish. If desired, serve with tomato sauce.
6 to 8 servings

Ossobuco
Italy

Translated into English, the name of this Italian dish (using veal knuckle) means "bone with hole". The explanation is simple. In northern Italy, the veal knuckle with bone is sliced lengthwise. Therefore the center of each slice of knuckle shows a piece of the tubelike bone, the bone with a hole. There is marrow in the hole which adds flavor enhancement to the dish.

1 veal knuckle. Flour
½ cup (⅛ liter or about ¼ pt.) olive oil
Salt. Pepper
½ cup (⅛ liter or about ¼ pt.) broth or bouillon
1 onion, chopped. 1 garlic clove, crushed
1 carrot, sliced. 1 piece leek
1 slice celery root or celeriac. 2 whole cloves
1 bay leaf. Pinch sage, thyme, rosemary
½ cup (⅛ liter or about ¼ pt.) white wine
1 can peeled whole tomatoes. Grated lemon peel

Have your butcher saw the veal knuckle into 4 or 5 slices. Dredge slices with flour. Heat several tablespoons oil in a skillet; add veal knuckle and brown well. Season with salt and pepper. Transfer meat to heatproof casserole or saucepot. Handle gently so the marrow remains in the cavity. Add the broth.

Add more oil to skillet, if needed; add onion, garlic, carrot, leek and celery. Cook and stir over medium heat about 5 minutes. Add the cloves, bay leaf and herbs. Pour in the wine and continue cooking until wine is almost evaporated. Stir in canned tomatoes and grated lemon. Cook several minutes. Turn mixture into casserole with the meat. Cover tightly and simmer until meat is tender. Remove knuckle slices to serving dish and keep hot.

Force vegetables in casserole through a sieve or food mill. If the resulting sauce is too thin, cook to reduce liquid. Add more seasoning, if needed. Pour over meat or serve sauce separately. Accompany with *rice* or *spaghetti* tossed with melted *butter* and topped with grated *Parmesan* or *Romano cheese*.

4 or 5 servings

59

Paella
Spain

Paella is a favorite dish that is served throughout Spain, especially in Valencia and environs. It is named after the large two-handled casserole-type pan in which it is traditionally cooked. The dish consists of a base of saffron-flavored rice to which may be added shellfish (shrimp, clams, lobsters), chicken, pork, chorizo and ham, along with any available vegetables.

½ cup (⅛ liter or about ¼ pt.) olive oil
½ lb. (250 g.) pork, cut in pieces
1 chicken (1¾ lbs. or 750 g.), cut up
2 onions, chopped. 1 garlic clove, crushed
¼ lb. (125 g.) uncooked ham, cut in strips
Salt. Pepper
4 cups (1 liter or about 2 pts.) broth or bouillon
2 pinches saffron. 1 bay leaf
1¾ cups (350 g. or ¾ lb.) uncooked rice
2 green peppers, cut in strips
4 tomatoes, peeled and cut up
1 cup green peas (fresh or frozen)
1 cup green beans (fresh or frozen)
1 small can mussels
¼ lb. (125 g.) cooked shrimp
2 oz. (65 g.) canned mushrooms. Cayenne pepper

Heat the oil in a large skillet (or paella pan if available). Add pork and chicken: cook about 15 minutes, or until chicken is browned on all sides. Add onion, garlic and ham; cook about 5 minutes longer. Season with salt and pepper. Add broth mixed with saffron and bay leaf; cook 30 minutes. Remove bay leaf and add rice. Cover and continue cooking 15 minutes.

Meanwhile, heat *1 or 2 tablespoons (15 or 30 milliliters) oil* in a heavy saucepan and add peppers and tomatoes. Cook about 5 minutes and add peas, beans and just enough *broth* or *water* to prevent vegetables from scorching. Cover and cook until vegetables are tender; add to rice mixture. Mix in the mussels, shrimp and mushrooms. Season to taste with *salt, pepper* and cayenne. Heat to serving temperature.
6 to 8 servings

Parisian Pepper Steak
France

The Pepper Steak, a beef fillet covered with coarsely crushed peppercorns, was in all probability created by a French cook. As the name Pepper Steak did not sound attractive enough, a menu-conscious gourmet added "Parisian". The classic French cuisine does list a pepper steak, though not necessarily a Parisian one.

The amount of crushed peppercorn used on the meat depends entirely on personal taste. As a guide, try two teaspoons for each side of a large steak.

Sirloin steak, cut 2 in. (5 cm.) thick; allow about ¾ lb. (375 g.) for each serving
1½ to 2 tablespoons (12 to 16 g.) peppercorns, crushed
Shortening or drippings. Salt
3 tablespoons (40 g. or 1½ oz.) butter or margarine
2 tablespoons chopped shallots. 2 small glasses brandy
Broth or bouillon. 1 dash Worcestershire sauce
1 dash tomato ketchup

Press coarsely crushed peppercorns into both sides of steak, so that the pepper clings to the meat. Heat several tablespoons shortening in a large heavy skillet; add steak and cook over high heat about 3 minutes, turning once. Season to taste with salt. Add butter and shallot to skillet and cook until meat is well browned. Flambé steak with brandy and arrange on a preheated platter.

Pour a small amount of broth or bouillon into skillet and add Worcestershire sauce; bring to boiling. Cook and stir for several minutes. Mix in ketchup. Serve sauce with the steaks. To carve, cut steak diagonally into thin slices.
About 4 servings

Pasta Asciutta
Italy

Italian pasta appears in so many different forms and shapes that it would be almost impossible to list them all. The term Pasta Asciutta designates all the pastas served "dry" with a sauce, while Pasta in Brodo means pasta served in broth. Often one can find that quite similar pastas have different names in various regions of Italy. Pasta Asciutta can be prepared in at least 100 different ways. The best known are Pasta Asciutta Bolognese (with ground meat sauce) and Pasta Asciutta Neapolitan (a meatless dish of spaghetti and tomato sauce). Here is a version of the latter dish.

1 onion, chopped. 1 garlic clove, crushed
5 tablespoons olive oil. ½ celery root (celeriac), grated
3 tomatoes, peeled and cut up
2 to 3 tablespoons sweet basil
2 cups (½ liter or about 1 pt.) broth or bouillon
Salt. Pepper. Nutmeg. Tomato ketchup
4 ripe olives, sliced. ½ lb. (250 g.) spaghetti

Brown onion and garlic in several tablespoons oil in a saucepot. Add celery root, tomatoes, and basil. Cook 3 to 5 minutes. Stir in broth and simmer over low heat 20 to 30 minutes.
While cooking, season with salt, pepper, nutmeg and ketchup to taste. Strain the mixture and add sliced olives.
Cook spaghetti in boiling salted water 8 to 12 minutes (or follow package directions). If desired, add 2 tablespoons cooking oil to the boiling salted water. Drain; toss spaghetti with hot sauce. Serve with fresh shredded Parmesan or Romano cheese.
4 servings

Peach Melba
France

This is an internationally known classic dessert. It was created by Auguste Escoffier, who at the time was chef de cuisine in a famous hotel in London. He named the dessert after an Australian soprano whose real name was Helen Porter Mitchell, but who called herself Nellie Melba in remembrance of her hometown, Melbourne. She must have been very proud of ''her'' Peach Melba, for in her elder years, in Australia, she is said to have given grand dinner parties that ended with the dessert. The original recipe called for peach halves that were poached in a sweet syrup, but modern recipes often use canned peaches, as in the following recipe.

4 portions vanilla ice cream
8 canned peach halves, drained
Raspberry purée (see below)
Whipped cream for garnishing
Pistachios or toasted slivered almonds (optional)

Place vanilla ice cream in stemmed dessert glasses. Cover with peach halves and top with raspberry purée. Garnish with whipped cream and nuts, if desired.
Raspberry Purée: Rinse 1½ cups (215 grams or 8 ounces) fully ripe raspberries and press through a coarse sieve or food mill. Sweeten with *2 to 4 tablespoons sugar* and chill thoroughly.
4 servings

Note: If fresh peaches are used, remove peel; halve peaches and remove pits. Prepare a syrup by boiling *1½ cups (⅜ liter or about ¾ pint) water* with *¾ to 1 cup (150 to 200 grams or 5 to 7 ounces) sugar* for 5 minutes. Add peach halves and cook only until peaches are tender but still firm. Remove peach halves from syrup and chill. Pear halves may be substituted for peaches, if desired.

63

Pichelsteiner (Stew)
Germany

This hearty meat and vegetable dish is quite typically German, but various interpretations of it appear in other countries around the world. Pichelsteiner usually combines two or more kinds of meat. In addition to potatoes, several other vegetables including a member of the cabbage family are used. It is thought that Pichelsteiner originated in Bavaria. Presumably, the dish was named for the mountain Buchelstein near the city of Regensburg.

½ lb. (250 g.) beef. ½ lb. (250 g.) pork
1 lb. (500 g.) potatoes. 3 oz. (80 g.) marrow or lard
1¾ lbs. (750 g.) mixed vegetables: carrots, celery, leek, cabbage, onions
Salt. Freshly ground pepper. Marjoram. Cumin seed
Parsley. 1 bay leaf
2 cups (½ liter or about 1 pt.) hot broth or bouillon

Cut meat and potatoes into pieces. Dice, slice or cut other vegetables into strips. Place slices of marrow on bottom of a heatproof casserole or Dutch oven or, if using lard instead of marrow, brush casserole with lard. Arrange alternate layers of meat, potatoes and the other vegetables in the casserole. Season each layer with salt, pepper and herbs. Add bay leaf.
Pour broth over all and bring to boiling over high heat. Cover tightly and cook gently over low heat about 1½ hours without stirring. Add more hot broth, if necessary to prevent scorching of vegetables.
About 6 servings

Note: If desired, brown the meat, a small amount at a time, in the lard before arranging layers in the casserole.

Pizza
Italy

This open-faced pie of Italian origin has many friends in the United States and is also becoming popular in central Europe. There are many recipes for pizza, but it usually consists of a breadlike crust topped with various mixtures the whole of which is baked and served warm.

Pizza Dough:
> 1 small cake (17 g.) fresh yeast. 1 teaspoon sugar
> 1 cup (¼ liter or about ½ pt.) lukewarm milk
> 2¼ cups (250 g. or 9 oz.) flour. ½ teaspoon salt
> 2 tablespoons oil or shortening

Topping:
> 3 tablespoons olive oil. 1 large (250 g. or 9 oz.) tomato
> 1½ cups (4 oz. or 100 g.) coarsely shredded
> Mozzarella cheese
> ¼ teaspoon salt. ⅛ teaspoon pepper
> 1 teaspoon oregano leaves (or use ½ teaspoon each
> oregano and thyme)
> 2 tablespoons shredded Parmesan cheese
> 1 small can mushrooms, drained and halved
> 6 thin slices lean bacon (partially fried and drained
> on absorbent paper)

Crumble yeast and mix with the sugar in a small mixer bowl. Add about half of the lukewarm milk. Mix well and beat in about ½ cup flour until smooth. Cover bowl and set aside in a warm place 30 minutes, or until mixture is bubbly. Beat in remaining milk, flour (with salt), and oil. Continue beating until smooth and satiny. Cover bowl and let rise in warm place until doubled in bulk.

Meanwhile, prepare topping. Heat oil in a small skillet; add cut-up tomatoes and cook 1 minute, stirring constantly; cool slightly.

When dough has doubled, turn onto a lightly oiled 12-inch (30-centimeter) pizza pan (one may use a large baking sheet). With oiled hands, press dough to cover bottom and sides of pizza pan. (When using baking sheet, press dough evenly into a 12-inch circle, building sides slightly.) Add the shredded Mozzarella cheese and the seasonings to the tomato mixture and spread mixture evenly over dough; sprinkle with Parmesan cheese and top with mushrooms and partially cooked bacon slices. Garnish with *parsley.*

Bake in a 425°F (220°C) oven 20 minutes, or until crust is golden.

One large pizza

Porterhouse Steak
England

Porterhouse is considered one of the choice (and expensive) cuts of steak. It is taken from the thick end of the short loin of beef and includes part of the tenderloin and fillet. It is at its best when cut very thick and grilled quickly over an open fire or under broiler heat. The following recipe calls for a well marbled steak, cut 2 to 2½ inches (5 to 6½ centimeters) thick. Panbroil it (as below), if you wish; or the steak may be placed in Claret Marinade and then grilled or broiled.

Lard or other fat. 2 lbs. (1 kg.) porterhouse steak
3 tablespoons (40 g. or 1½ oz.) butter
Salt. Pepper
Cooked vegetables (peas, carrots, cauliflower, asparagus spears, green beans, tomatoes)
Melted butter. Lemon juice. Parsley sprigs

Heat a large heavy skillet, adding a small amount of lard. Add the steak and brown quickly on both sides over high heat. Lower heat and continue until meat is cooked as preferred, adding butter as needed. Season with salt and pepper. Place steak on a preheated platter and surround it with cooked vegetables that have been tossed with melted butter blended with lemon juice. Garnish with parsley.
4 servings

Grilled Claret Steak: Marinate thick steak in Claret *Marinade* (see below) several hours before grilling. Turn steak occasionally while marinating. When ready to cook, remove from marinade and place on a grill (or under broiler) 3 to 4 inches (8 to 10 centimeters) from the heat. Grill until well browned on both sides, brushing frequently with the marinade. Season with *salt* and *pepper*. Grill 6 to 7 minutes on each side for a rare steak.

Claret Marinade: Combine ½ cup (⅛ liter or about ¼ pint) each *claret* and *olive oil, 1 large clove garlic*, crushed, 2 or 3 drops Tabasco, ¼ teaspoon each *dry mustard* and *nutmeg*.

Quiche Lorraine
France

Quiche Lorraine, probably originating in Alsace-Lorraine, has bit of bacon (or ham) and cheese added to the custard. Sometimes crab meat, salmon, sliced onion and other ingredients are added and the quiche is served as hors d'oeuvres or as a luncheon or supper entrée along with a crisp salad.

7 oz. (200 g.) flour. ½ teaspoon salt
3 tablespoons water. 5 oz. (150 g.) butter
Bread crumbs. 4 eggs
½ cup (115 g.) thick sour cream

5 oz. (150 g.) lean bacon or ham, diced
9 oz. (250 g.) Swiss cheese, diced
Parsley, chopped. 1 teaspoon paprika

Mix flour and salt in a bowl. Make a well in center and add water. Using a pastry blender, cut in butter in small pieces. Mix well until dough can be formed into a smooth ball. Cover; chill 1 hour. Roll out dough on floured canvas into a round 12 inches in diameter Line a 10-inch flan pan with pastry, turning edge of dough under and flute the edge. Sprinkle with 1 tablespoon fine bread crumbs. Beat eggs slightly and beat in sour cream. Add diced bacon (or ham), cheese, parsley and paprika. Turn into pastry shell. Bake in a 400-425°F (200-220°C) oven 25 to 30 minutes. Serve warm.
One 10-inch Quiche

67

Ragoût Fin
France

The classic French dish Ragoût Fin is usually served in puff-paste patty shells.

1 small veal tongue. Soup greens
1 veal sweetbread. 1 tablespoon lemon juice
2 oz. (50 g.) butter
2 oz. (50 g.) flour
2 egg yolks, slightly beaten
1 anchovy fillet, chopped. 1 teaspoon capers

1 small can mushrooms, drained and chopped

Cover tongue and soup greens with *salted water* in a kettle. Cook, covered, until tongue is tender. Let cool in the broth, then remove skin from tongue. Remove membrane from sweetbread and simmer in enough *salted water* to cover (lemon juice added) until tender. Cut sweetbread and tongue into cubes. Melt butter in a skillet; stir in flour. Cook and stir until flour is lightly browned. Blend in *3 cups (¾ liter or 1½ pints) broth* or *bouillon* and bring to boiling, stirring constantly until sauce is thickened. Blend egg yolks into sauce. Add anchovy fillet, capers, mushrooms and meat. Serve hot.   *4 servings*

68

Ratatouille
France

Ratatouille is a specialty of Provence with obvious overtones of the Italian and Spanish cuisine. The dish is simply a vegetable stew or a combination of vegetables such as eggplant, onion, tomatoes, green peppers and even pumpkin all cooked in a casserole. However, in some versions of this dish each vegetable is sautéed or cooked in water separately and combined before serving. The vegetables are well seasoned with garlic and sometimes with herbs such as basil, thyme and marjoram.

3 green peppers, cut in strips. 3 small eggplants
3 zucchini (courgettes). 4 tomatoes
4 tablespoons olive oil. 1 large onion, sliced
1 large clove garlic, crushed. Salt
Freshly ground black pepper. ½ bay leaf
3 sprigs parsley, chopped
Grated fresh Parmesan cheese. Butter or margarine

Clean peppers and cut into strips. Pare eggplants, quarter lengthwise and slice. Scrub zucchini thoroughly and cut into ¼-inch (½-centimeter) slices.

Lightly salt the eggplant and zucchini slices, arrange them in layers in bowl and weigh down with a heavy plate or platter. Let stand about 30 minutes, then dry slices on absorbent paper. Peel and coarsely chop (or quarter) tomatoes.

Heat some of the oil in a large skillet or heatproof casserole; add onion, garlic, salt and black pepper. Cook 3 to 5 minutes over high heat. Add sliced eggplant and zucchini and cook 2 or 3 minutes longer, adding more oil as needed. Add tomatoes and season to taste with salt and pepper; add bay leaf and parsley. Cover tightly and cook until vegetables are just tender (not mushy). Sprinkle generously with grated cheese. Dot with butter and place under broiler heat a few minutes until top is lightly browned.

About 6 servings

Roast
Saddle of Venison
England

This game specialty is attributed to the English cuisine by virtue of the Cumberland sauce and not because of the venison, which is usually prepared in the same manner everywhere. The sauce was named in honor of Ernest August, Duke of Cumberland (1845-1923). It consists of currant jelly and wine (usually port) subtly seasoned with mustard and citrus juice and peel and is often served with ham and game.

4½ lbs. (2 kg.) saddle of venison
3 to 4 cups (¾ to 1 liter or about 1½ to 2 pts.) buttermilk
3 juniper berries. 1 bay leaf. 5 peppercorns
3 lemon slices. Salt. Pepper
6 to 8 slices (225 g. or 8 oz.) bacon
8 tablespoons (100 g. or 4 oz.) butter or margarine, melted

Cumberland Sauce
Peel of 1 orange, finely slivered. 3 tablespoons red wine
¾ cup (200 g. or 7 oz.) red currant jelly
1 teaspoon dry mustard. Salt
2 to 3 tablespoons lemon juice

Remove skin from saddle of venison. Marinate for 2 days in a sauce of buttermilk, juniper berries, bay leaf, peppercorns and lemon slices. Turn meat occasionally. Drain and pat dry. Rub venison with salt and pepper. Lard the meat with bacon slices (see note). Place in a shallow roasting pan; brush generously with melted butter and place in a moderate oven (350°F or 180°C) 40 to 60 minutes. The roast should be well browned on the outside and remain pink inside. Baste occasionally with hot water or drippings in pan. During the last 10 minutes of the cooking time, remove bacon slices so that meat may brown completely. Let roast stand a few minutes before serving. Carefully carve meat along the center of the bone. Cut diagonally and replace meat on the ridge.

Cumberland Sauce: Combine orange peel with the wine in a small saucepan. Simmer for 15 minutes and blend in the remaining ingredients. Serve in a sauceboat at room temperature.
6 to 8 servings

Note: To lard the meat, cut deep slits in the surface and insert strips of bacon into the flesh.

70

Rice Trauttmansdorff
Austria

The Trauttmansdorffs are an old Austrian family of nobility from the Wienerwald. One member of the family fought in the battle of the Champ de Mars and another played an important part in setting up the Peace of Westphalia which ended the Thirty Years' War.

The creator of this delicious creamy rice dish is unknown but it was probably named for Ferdinand, Count of Trauttmansdorff, who, as diplomat and ambassador, was known in many European capitals. Returning to Vienna at the age of forty-seven, he became vice-president and later president of the House of Lords.

⅔ cup (125 g. or 4½ oz.) long-grain rice
3 cups (¾ liter or about 1½ pts.) milk
¼ teaspoon salt. ⅓ cup (70 g. or 2½ oz.) sugar
1 piece (about 1 in.) vanilla bean
2 env. (14 g. or ½ oz.) unflavored gelatin
1 cup (¼ liter or about ½ pt.) whipping cream
2 tablespoons maraschino
⅔ cup (125 g. or 4½ oz.) candied fruit

Combine rice, 2½ cups (⅝ liter or about 1¼ pints) of the milk, salt, sugar and piece of vanilla bean in a heavy saucepan. Cover tightly and cook over low heat until rice kernels are soft and liquid is absorbed. Remove vanilla bean and set rice aside to cool.

Soften gelatin in remaining milk. Heat over hot water until gelatin is completely dissolved. Let cool slightly.

Beat cream until soft peaks are formed, blending in the maraschino the last few seconds. Coarsely chop the candied fruit. Combine the dissolved gelatin with rice, mix well and add the candied fruit. Fold in the whipped cream (sweetened with a little sugar, if desired). Turn into a pudding mold. Chill until firm.

When ready to serve, unmold dessert onto a serving plate and garnish with additional candied fruit. Serve with a wine or fruit sauce.

About 6 servings

Sauerbraten (Rhineland Style)
Germany

Recent polls indicate that Sauerbraten is the favorite dish of the Germans. In most regions of Germany, the beef is marinated in a vinegar-onion-spice mixture and allowed to stand in the refrigerator for several days or even a week. When ready to use, the meat is cooked like a pot roast in the marinade sauce. In the Rhineland, the sauce is thickened by adding crumbled gingersnaps and golden raisins during the last few minutes of cooking. The meat must be cooked until very tender. If desired, bacon slices may be spread over surface while cooking.

2 lbs. (1 kg.) boneless beef roast, preferably top or bottom round or rump
6 tablespoons lard

Marinade:

2 cups (½ liter or about 1 pt.) water
1 cup (¼ liter or about ½ pt.) vinegar
1 teaspoon salt. 2 onions. 1 carrot. 5 peppercorns
2 whole cloves. 1 bay leaf. 2 juniper berries

Sauce:

¾ cup (125 g. or 4½ oz.) golden raisins
5 or 6 (about 75 g.) gingersnaps, crumbled
1 tablespoon thick unsweetened apple juice or apple syrup
Salt. Pepper
1 cup (¼ liter or about ½ pt.) thick sour cream

Combine ingredients for marinade in a saucepan; bring to boiling. Set aside to cool. Place meat in an earthenware pot and pour cooled marinade over it. Marinate several days, turning occasionally. Remove meat and pat dry.

Strain the marinade for sauce. Heat lard in heavy saucepot or Dutch oven; add meat and brown well on all sides. Add the strained marinade, cover and cook slowly 1½ hours, or until meat is tender, basting frequently. Add raisins and gingersnap crumbs about 15 minutes before end of cooking time. Add the apple juice (or syrup) and more seasoning if needed. Stir in the sour cream.

Serve Sauerbraten with potato dumplings or potato pancakes (Kartoffelpuffer) and applesauce.

4 to 6 servings

Risotto
Italy

Risotto is not just an ordinary cooked rice dish. First of all, for best results one should use the soft round-grain rice, not the hard long-grain kernels. Secondly, the rice should be sautéed in olive oil before the cooking liquid (usually broth) is added. Onion is often added, as are saffron and Parmesan cheese. Or, for a complete one-dish meal, one may add mushrooms, mussels, shrimp, tomatoes, green peppers, cooked chicken and other flavor-compatible ingredients.

1 onion, finely chopped. 4 tablespoons olive oil
1¼ cups (250 g. or 9 oz.) round-grain rice
2 cups (½ liter or about 1 pt.) broth or bouillon
1 lb. (500 g.) cooked beef, diced. 1 cup fresh peas
2 eggs. ½ cup (⅛ liter or about ¼ pt.) milk
3½ oz. (100 g.) shredded Italian cheese. Salt. Pepper
Marjoram, thyme

Cook onion in hot oil in skillet or saucepan about 3 minutes. Add rice and cook, stirring frequently, until rice is lightly browned. Add broth and bring rice to boiling, stirring constantly. Cover tightly and cook over low heat 18 minutes, or until rice kernels are soft and liquid is absorbed. (Add more broth, if needed.) Mix rice with the meat and peas. Transfer to a greased baking dish.

Lightly beat eggs with the milk and stir in the cheese. Season with salt, pepper, marjoram and thyme. Pour this egg-milk mixture over the rice. Bake in a moderate oven (350°F or 180°C) 12 to 15 minutes.

6 to 8 servings

Sacher Torte
Austria

Edward Sacher, Prince Metternich's cook, is said to have created this rich chocolate cake in 1832.

The cake is glazed with puréed apricot preserves and topped with a chocolate frosting. It is often served Vienna-style with whipped cream (mit schlag). There are many recipes claiming to be the "original" Sacher Torte from the house of Sacher, the Austrian family of noted hotelkeepers - and restaurateurs. Today, one may still dine at the Sacher Hotel in Vienna, where the famous torte is served. Here is our favorite recipe.

8 oz. (225 g.) unsweetened chocolate
½ lb. (200 g.) butter
2 cups (240 g. or 9 oz.) confectioners' sugar
8 egg yolks, well beaten. ⅔ cup fine dry bread crumbs
8 egg whites. ⅛ teaspoon salt
⅔ cup (200 g. or 7 oz.) apricot preserves,
puréed and heated
Sugar icing for decoration

Grease bottom of a 9-inch (23-centimeter) springform pan and line bottom with waxed paper.

Melt chocolate and set aside to cool.

Cream butter in large mixer bowl until softened; beat in 1 cup of the sugar until fluffy. Gradually add egg yolks, beating well after each addition. Blend in chocolate and crumbs.

Beat egg whites with salt until frothy. Add remaining cup of sugar, several tablespoons at a time, beating constantly until peaks are formed. Spread egg yolk mixture over egg whites and gently fold together. Turn batter into the pan.

Bake in a moderate oven (350°F or 180°C) 50 to 60 minutes. Remove from oven and place on a wire rack several minutes. Then invert pan on rack and allow cake to cool completely. Carefully loosen sides with spatula and remove cake from pan. Peel off waxed paper.

Spread torte with heated puréed apricot preserves. Set aside a few minutes, then cover torte with Chocolate Frosting.

Chocolate Frosting: Partially melt *3 ounces (85 grams) semi-sweet chocolate,* remove from heat and stir until melted. Add *4 ounces (100 grams) unsalted butter* and stir until melted.

If desired, cut the surface of the Sacher Torte into 12 parts and inscribe each with the name "Sacher" with sugar icing.

12 servings

74

Saltimbocca
Italy

This ham and veal dish is typically Italian: it uses sage as the seasoning, it is fried in oil and the dish consists of relatively small portions of meat. In Italy, a meal generally begins with a pasta dish, such as Pasta Asciutta, which alone is quite satisfying. So the main dish (usually meat) that follows should be more delicate than heavy. The pieces of meat in this recipe are bite-sized and nobody has to struggle with them. They, so to speak, "jump in the mouth" which is the literal translation of Saltimbocca.

4 large, thinly sliced veal cutlets. Salt. Pepper
2 tablespoons flour
4 large, very thin slices uncooked ham
Fresh sage leaves. Olive oil. 1 small glass Marsala

Place veal slices on a cutting board and beat until very thin with a meat hammer; divide each slice into 2 or 3 pieces. Season meat with salt and pepper and dredge with flour. Cut the ham into pieces the same size as veal. Place a sage leaf on each piece of veal and top with a slice of ham. Secure with wooden pick.

Heat several tablespoons olive oil in skillet; add the meat and sauté slowly until golden brown on both sides. Remove meat to heated platter and keep warm. Scrape drippings from bottom of pan; add the wine and simmer gently several minutes. Pour over the meat. Serve with *fried semolina slices*. *To prepare semolina:* Cook *semolina* (or cornmeal) with *milk* until very thick. Season with *salt* and turn into a small loaf pan or spread on a shallow plate. Allow to chill until firm, then turn out onto cutting board and slice ½ inch thick. If chilled on a platter, turn onto board and cut into rectangles. Coat with *bread crumbs* and fry in hot *oil* (or other shortening) until golden.
4 servings

Salzburger Nockerln
Austria

''He who dislikes Salzburger Nockerln has no claim to being an Austrian'', they say in Salzburg. Furthermore, the housewife who cannot bake Nockerln is considered an untalented cook. Baking Nockerln is indeed no easy art. This can be confirmed by all those cooks who have begun their work with all good intentions and are rewarded for their efforts with nothing but a soggy flat pancake.

Nockerln is the German term for light dumplings made in various ways. The famous Salzburger Nockerln consists mostly of egg foam and has very little flour in it. To avoid the collapse of this fluffy mixture, one must follow directions explicitly.

The famous Nockerln is supposed to have been created at the beginning of the seventeenth century under the aegis of Dietrich of Raitenau, who was the archbishop of Salzburg. He loved power, splendor and fluffy sweet desserts.

4 egg whites. ¼ cup (50 g. or 2 oz.) fine granulated sugar
1 tablespoon (10 g. or ½ oz.) vanilla-flavored sugar
3 tablespoons (40 g. or 1½ oz.) unsalted butter
3 egg yolks. 3 tablespoons (20 g. or ¾ oz.) flour

Start preheating oven to very hot (450°F or 230°C).

Beat egg whites until soft peaks are formed; beat in sugar and vanilla sugar, 2 tablespoons at a time. Continue beating until very stiff peaks are formed.

Put the butter into a round shallow baking dish or skillet; set on low rack in oven until butter is melted.

Meanwhile, beat egg yolks until thick. Fold about 3 tablespoons of the beaten egg whites into egg yolks, then fold into remaining egg whites. Continue folding gently, sifting the flour over mixture during folding process.

Remove heated dish from oven and gently spoon egg mixture into 4 mounds in dish. Return to oven and bake until lightly browned, about 8 minutes. Serve immediately, protecting the dish from draft or high temperature changes. Sprinkle baked Nockerln with *confectioners' sugar* or *vanilla-flavored sugar*.
4 servings

Sarma
Yugoslavia

This dish (also called Sarmi or Sarmale) originated in Turkey but is known in all Balkan countries. It consists of cabbage (or grape) leaves filled with a savory meat and rice stuffing and is cooked in a well seasoned sauce.

1 head cabbage. 2 onions, chopped
3 tablespoons (40 g. or 1½ oz.) butter
1 garlic clove, crushed
12 oz. (350 g.) ground meat
1 cup (200 g. or 7 oz.) cooked rice
½ cup (75 g. or 2½ oz.) raisins (optional)
Salt. Pepper. Chopped parsley
1 egg, slightly beaten. Buttered crumbs

Cook cabbage in boiling *salted water* until tender. Carefully remove 8 large leaves. Cook onion in butter in skillet about 3 minutes; add garlic and meat and cook until meat is browned. Mix in rice and raisins (if used); season to taste and set aside to cool. Add parsley and egg. Spread mixture over cabbage leaves and roll up. Transfer to a heatproof casserole. Add about *1 cup (¼ liter or about ½ pint) broth or tomato sauce;* cover casserole and cook gently about 5 minutes. Top with crumbs and place under broiler until crumbs are golden.
About 6 servings

77

Sataras
Yugoslavia

Sataras is a stewlike meat and vegetable dish that comes from Yugoslavia; it is also known in Bulgaria. Originally, it was prepared outdoors by shepherds.

½ lb. (250 g.) beef. ½ lb. (250 g.) mutton
½ lb. (250 g.) pork
⅓ cup (70 g. or 2½ oz.) butter or margarine
3 onions, chopped. 1 garlic clove, crushed
1 tablespoon paprika. Salt

1 teaspoon cumin seed, crushed
3 medium tomatoes, chopped
4 green peppers, chopped
½ cup (115 g. or about ¼ pt.) thick sour cream

Cut the meat into 1½-inch cubes; brown on all sides in heated fat in skillet. Add onion and garlic; sprinkle with paprika; continue cooking 3 or 4 minutes. Add a small amount of *water*. Season to taste with salt and add cumin. Cover and simmer 40 to 50 minutes. Add chopped tomato and green pepper; cover casserole and cook until done. Add more seasoning, if needed. Remove from heat and blend in sour cream. Serve with rice and fresh vegetable salad.
6 to 8 servings

78

Savarin
France

Jean Antheime Brillat-Savarin, for whom this cakelike dessert was named, was a renowned gourmet. His *Physiology of Taste* was published in 1825 and even today is considered the standard work on epicurean dining. The book contains only a few recipes, but is renowned for such epigrams as, "The discovery of a new dish is of greater importance to the happiness of mankind than the discovery of a new star". Brillat-Savarin was right.

2½ cups (300 g. or 11 oz.) flour
1 small cake (17 g.) fresh yeast
½ cup (⅛ liter or about ¼ pt.) milk, warmed
½ cup (100 g. or 3½ oz.) sugar
1 tablespoon vanilla-flavored sugar
8 tablespoons butter, softened
½ teaspoon salt. 2 eggs, well beaten

Filling:

1½ cups (300 g. or 10½ oz.) sugar
1 cup (¼ liter or about ½ pt.) water
3 small glasses pflümli. 2 small glasses maraschino
1¾ lbs. (750 g.) cooked pitted prune plums, well drained
1 cup (¼ liter or about ½ pt.) whipping cream

Make a well in the center of flour in a bowl. Crumble in yeast and add half of the milk and 1 teaspoon sugar. Stir until yeast is dissolved. Mix in enough flour to make a soft sponge. Cover and let rise in warm place 30 minutes. Meanwhile, beat butter with remaining sugar until creamy. Beat remaining milk, salt and the eggs into yeast mixture, then beat in butter mixture a little at a time. Cover; let rise in warm place until doubled. Turn into a well greased 6-cup (1½ liter) ring mold, spreading evenly. Let dough rise to top of mold.

Bake in a moderately hot oven (375°F or 190°C) about 30 minutes. Let cool slightly, then invert on a plate. Remove the mold from cake.

Meanwhile, combine sugar and water in a saucepan and boil 5 minutes. Remove from heat and stir in the two liqueurs. If desired, pour the syrup over drained prune plums in a bowl; set aside 30 minutes. Drain fruit; reheat the syrup.

Prick Savarin with wooden skewer and pour syrup over it. Spoon syrup over cake until syrup is absorbed. Fill center of Savarin with whipped cream and cooked prune plums (or other fruit). Garnish with whipped cream rosettes sprinkled with chopped *pistachio* nuts.

8 to 10 servings

Shaslik
(Shish Kebab)
Soviet Union, Orient

A kebab is meat, especially lamb, cut in cubes. The meat is often marinated in a well seasoned mixture to achieve a more interesting flavor and broiled on a shish, the Turkish word for skewer. Even the oldest German cookbook from the fourteenth century suggested the use of a skewer "eines vingers lanc" (the length of a finger) to roast meat.

This method of cooking meat was largely forgotten except in southern Russia and in the countries under Turkish influence. The Armenians, for example, often served shaslyk (as they are called in Armenia) at their outdoor picnics, grilling them over an open fire, using grapevines for their fire. The lamb was usually slaughtered at the site of their outing. When meat cooked on skewers became a part of European cuisine, it was known as Russian shashlik or Turkish Shish Kebab.

1 tablespoon olive oil. ½ teaspoon sugar
Juice of 1 lemon. Salt
Freshly ground black pepper. 1 lb. (500 g.) lamb or mutton
¼ lb. (125 g.) lean smoked bacon, sliced
2 onions, thickly sliced. Oil for frying

Combine olive oil, sugar, lemon juice, salt and pepper in a bowl; beat thoroughly with rotary beater. Cut the meat in cubes, add to the bowl and marinate for several hours, turning meat frequently.

When ready to cook, insert meat on skewer, alternating with onions and bacon slices. Brush again with oil and cook on a grill over an open fire or under broiler heat.

Serve with curried rice and tomato or green pepper salad.

4 to 6 servings

Variation: Substitute for lamb either pork, beef or veal, or several of these meats. Alternate meat on the skewer with any of the following: slices of *liver, kidney, sausage, cucumber* or *tomato;* pieces of *green pepper,* thick slices of *apple* or *orange, mushrooms,* mixed *pickles,* or *olives.*

Turtle Soup
England

Turtle Soup has long been a national favorite in England, and in the British Empire there was a constant supply of turtles available for soup. Also, Turtle Soup in cans has been marketed for some time in England.

Nowadays, the kind of turtle used for soups is bred in the tropical or subtropical zones of the United States and Japan. In most private households or even restaurants today, no one is likely to kill a turtle himself in order to prepare the soup. It is far more convenient and timesaving to buy canned or frozen turtle meat.

Canned Turtle Soup, to simply heat and serve, can be glamorized in the "Lady Curzon" manner, as described below. Lady Curzon was the wife of the British Viceroy of India, the Marquess Curzon of Kedleston (1859-1925).

1 can turtle soup. 4 tablespoons sherry
4 tablespoons whipped cream. 1 teaspoon curry powder

Heat the canned turtle soup, but do not bring to boiling. Pour soup into bouillon cups or individual bowls. Stir one table-spoon of sherry into each serving. Top with whipped cream and sprinkle with curry powder. Serve immediately.
4 servings

Note: If desired, serve the soup in heat-resistant cups or bowls and set under the broiler until tops are lightly browned (watch carefully to avoid overbrowning).

Turtle Soup (using fresh or frozen turtle meat):
In a saucepot, combine *1 cup (125 grams or 4½ ounces) diced turtle meat,* 5 to 6 cups (1¼ to 1½ liters or 2½ to 3 pints) beef broth or bouillon, 1 bay leaf, 1 tablespoon lemon juice, and *salt* and *pepper* to taste. Bring to boiling; cover and cook over low heat until turtle meat is tender. Serve in cups or bowls. Pour a little *sherry* into each serving and garnish with *chopped hard-cooked egg white.*
About 6 servings

Schnitzel Holstein
Germany

This feast of a veal cutlet owes its name to the councillor Friedrich von Holstein (1837-1909), who is known in history as the influential "Grey Eminence" at the Prussian court. The ingenious diplomat was not fond of appearing in public and preferred to operate in the background to achieve whatever he wanted. There is reason to believe that he might have been involved in the downfall of Bismarck. But even during Chancellor von Bulow's time the strange councillor was influential enough to make his presence felt. Obviously, he understood quite a lot about food. "His" cutlet was prepared according to his directions by the chef de cuisine of the Restaurant Borchardt of the Französische Strasse in Berlin. One might add that the name of the veal recipe has nothing to do with the territory of Holstein.

4 veal cutlets. 1 tablespoon flour
Lard or other shortening. Salt. Pepper
4 eggs. 2 anchovy fillets. 2 teaspoons capers
4 slices white bread, toasted
2 tablespoons butter or margarine
4 sardines in oil. 4 slices smoked salmon
1 small can caviar

Dredge veal cutlets with flour and fry them in hot lard in a skillet. Season with salt and pepper. Arrange on a preheated platter and keep warm.
Fry 4 eggs and top each cutlet with an egg. Garnish with anchovy fillets and capers.
Butter toast and cut into small triangles. Cover with sardines, smoked salmon and caviar. Arrange around the cutlets.
If desired, the cutlets may be served with buttered green beans, sautéed mushrooms and German-fried potatoes.
4 servings

Sweet and Sour Pork
China

Pork is, no doubt, the favorite meat in the Chinese diet. The numerous and epicurean ways of cooking it are truly remarkable. Although the recipe below has been adapted for European tastes, sweet and sour pork is traditionally a Far Eastern dish.

¾ lb. (350 g.) lean boneless pork
1 small glass prunelle (liqueur)
1 tablespoon soy sauce. Salt
Fat for deep-frying, heated to 350-375° (180-190°C)

Batter:

1 egg, slightly beaten. ½ teaspoon sugar
½ cup (⅛ liter or about ¼ pt.) light beer
1 teaspoon oil. 1 cup (125 g. or 4½ oz.) flour
2 tablespoons (18 g.) cornstarch. ½ teaspoon salt

Sauce:

2 tablespoons peanut oil. 1 large garlic clove, crushed
1 green pepper, cut in small pieces
1 carrot, cut in julienne strips
½ cup (⅛ liter or about ¼ pt.) chicken broth
2 tablespoons honey; or use 3 tablespoons sugar
1 tablespoon soy sauce. 3 tablespoons red wine vinegar
1 piece crystallized ginger, minced
4 or 5 cocktail onions (optional)
1 tablespoon (9 g.) cornstarch

Cut pork into bite-sized pieces. Marinate several hours in a mixture of prunelle, soy sauce and salt.

For batter, combine all the ingredients in a bowl and beat until smooth. Let rest 30 minutes.

For sauce, heat oil in saucepan or skillet; add the garlic and cook ½ minute. Then add the green pepper and carrot and sauté about 3 minutes, stirring constantly. Stir in a mixture of the broth, honey (or sugar), soy sauce, wine vinegar and minced ginger. Simmer 8 to 10 minutes. Add onions (if used). Thicken sauce with cornstarch mixed with several tablespoons *cold water*.

When ready to serve, dip pieces of pork in batter and deep-fry in hot fat until golden. Serve meat with sauce and rice.
4 servings

Sole Marguery
France

No other fish has inspired famous continental chefs as much as sole. Hundreds of sole recipes are to be found, especially in the French cuisine.

Sole belongs to the family called flounder. European sole is highly regarded and is far better, and far more expensive, than the sole found in American waters. Sole Marguery was named for the Parisian restaurant Marguery on the Boulevard Bonne-Nouvelle, where the restaurateur conceived the idea of combining sole with mussels and shrimps. Today Sole Marguery appears on menus everywhere.

4 fillets of sole
½ cup (⅛ liter or about ¼ pt.) white wine
Soup greens (see note with Bollito Misto)
Salt and pepper. 2 teaspoons (6 g.) cornstarch
1 egg yolk, slightly beaten
4 tablespoons cream or evaporated milk
24 canned mussels. 1 small can shrimps

Prepare the fish fillets and put heads, bones and skin for stock into a saucepan.

For stock: Cover the contents of saucepan with about *2 cups (½ liter or about 1 pint) water.* Add wine and soup greens. Cover and cook gently about 30 minutes. Strain stock.

Sprinkle fillets with salt and pepper.

Generously grease a heatproof dish with butter; add fish fillets and pour in the strained stock. Cover and simmer about 8 minutes. Remove poached fillets to serving dish and keep warm.

Thicken stock with cornstarch mixed with a little cold *water.* Blend in egg yolk and cream and season to taste. Add canned mussels and shrimps, drained, to the sauce and heat thoroughly. Spoon the sauce over the fillets and serve with puff pastry rounds or fluffy rice.

4 servings

84

Smorrebrod
Denmark

The Danish word *Smorrebrod* literally translated means buttered bread. The word also refers to a famous open-faced sandwich . . . and what sandwiches the Danes can create! Thin buttered slices of bread are topped with colorful combinations of several foods such as meat, pieces of chicken, smoked eel and pâté de foie gras, diced ham and cheese, hard-cooked eggs, cucumbers and so on. Foot-long Smorrebrod menu cards can be found in many Danish restaurants. Homemakers have been known to have at least one hundred Smorrebrod recipes in their heads.

Denmark's neighbor, Sweden, another master of the cold buffet, has similar plates, called Smörgasbord.

Breads:
> Sandwich loaf (white bread), country-style bread, whole wheat bread, or pumpernickel.

Spreads:
> Softened butter combined with lemon juice, herbs, mustard, paprika, curry powder, flaked crab meat, lobster, or tuna.

Sauces:
> Mayonnaise, remoulade, commercial dressings, spicy sauces.

Toppings:
> Sausages and meats, pâtés, marinated fish, crab meat, shrimps and lobster meat, fresh and cooked vegetables, salads, all kinds of cheeses.

Suggestions for Smorrebrod:
1. Shrimp with mayonnaise, lemon wedges, chopped watercress.
2. Smoked eel, cold scrambled egg.
3. Pâté de foie, smoked tongue.
4. Fried liver, slices of bacon, fried onion rings, apple slices.
5. Fried fish fillet, remoulade sauce.
6. Celery salad, fried pieces of chicken, jelly.
7. Slices of roast beef, remoulade sauce, mixed pickles.
8. Asparagus, smoked meat, chopped parsley.
9. Blue cheese, raw egg yolk, slices of radish.
10. Caviar, chopped hard-cooked egg white, lemon wedges.
11. Rye bread, butter, pickled herring, onion and capers.
12. Thick slice of liver pâté on white or rye bread, crowned with sautéed mushrooms.
13. Cold chicken breast with cucumber slices vinaigrette (combine *vinegar, salt, pepper* and *sugar* to taste).
14. Warm scrambled eggs spooned on rye bread, topped with crisp fried bacon and cocktail sausages.
15. Thinly sliced, slightly warm roast pork on rye bread slices, topped with red cabbage and garnished with cooked apple slices and prunes.

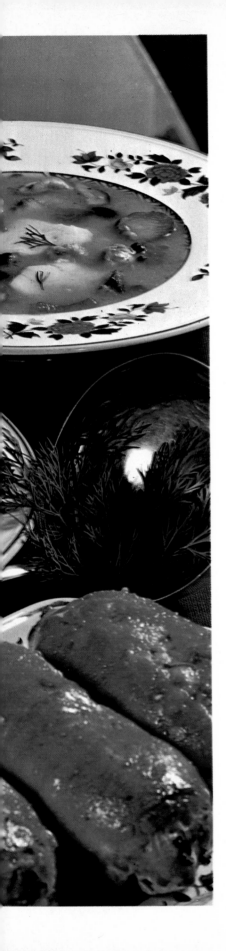

Solianka
Soviet Union

This hearty soup, along with Borscht, is a favorite Russian preparation. Solianka may be prepared in many different ways; with sauerkraut and fish, or with cabbage and leftover roast, as a thin or thick soup, or as a copious meal-in-a-dish (or thin stew) cooked in the oven.

The following recipe for Solianka will have international appeal, as it uses a combination of fish and shellfish and is subtly flavored.

1 lb. (500 g.) fish
Soup greens (see note with Bollito Misto)
4 tablespoons butter or margarine
1 medium onion, thinly sliced
1 medium cucumber, peeled and coarsely chopped
(seeds removed)
2 medium tomatoes, peeled and cut in pieces
Salt. White pepper
2½ oz. (75 g.) shrimp (or lobster)
2½ oz. (75 g.) canned mussels. 1 gherkin, thinly sliced
5 pitted ripe olives, sliced. 1 teaspoon capers
Thin lemon slices (halved). Fresh dill

Prepare fish fillets.

To prepare fish broth: cover fish heads, bones and fins with boiling *salted water* in a saucepot. Add soup greens and cook 45 to 50 minutes. Strain broth.

Cook sliced onion in heated butter in a saucepot about 8 minutes; do not brown. Add cucumber and tomato and simmer 10 minutes. Pour in strained stock and season to taste with salt and white pepper. Heat to boiling, add fish (cut in pieces) and cook gently until fish is done. Add shrimp (or pieces of lobster meat) and mussels and simmer several minutes. Mix in the sliced gherkins, ripe olives and capers. Add thin lemon slices (halved) and fresh dill. If desired, garnish with thick sour cream or serve cream separately.

About 4 servings

Soufflé
Fürst Pückler
Germany

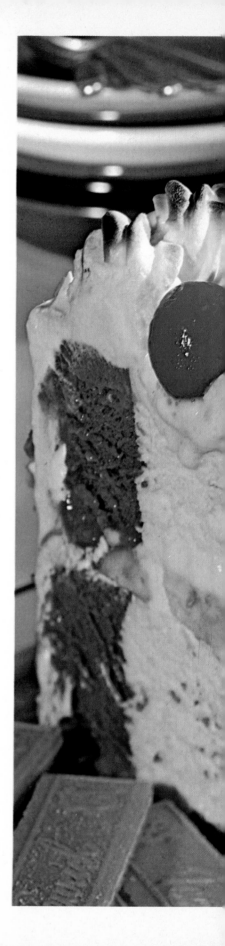

One version of this specialty is a delicate soufflé-type dessert consisting mainly of beaten egg whites, baked in the oven and served hot. Another interpretation, as described below, consists of a "surprise soufflé" made with ice cream. The ice cream is hidden under a fluffy meringue baked quickly (or broiled) at high temperature until golden and served immediately before the ice cream begins to melt.

The creation is named in honor of the gourmet, landscape gardener and adventurer, Herman, Prince of Pückler-Muskau, who lived in the eighteenth century.

A well known adaptation of this creation, served often in the United States and called Baked Alaska, is made with a sponge or pound cake "base" topped with a brick of ice cream, which is covered with meringue and quickly browned in the oven.

> 4 egg whites. 14 tablespoons sugar
> Grated peel of 1 lemon (optional)
> 2 pkgs. (bricks) ice cream (chocolate, vanilla or
> strawberry), frozen very firm
> 2 bananas, halved lengthwise
> 2 tablespoons slivered almonds. Maraschino cherries

Beat egg whites until frothy; add sugar, several tablespoons at a time, and beat well. Continue beating until very stiff peaks are formed; quickly beat in grated lemon peel (if used). Place one package of the ice cream on a wooden board; cover with the halved bananas and top with the second package of ice cream. Coat sides and surface of loaf with the meringue and decorate with some of the meringue put· through a pastry bag with decorating tube. Sprinkle sides with slivered almonds.

Place in preheated 500°F (260°C) oven only until golden (or broil quickly under broiler, about 7 inches from heat source). Garnish loaf with the cherries and serve immediately with ladyfingers or wafers. If not served immediately, store dessert in freezer to avoid melting of ice cream.

About 8 servings

Sukiyaki
Japan

It is traditional in Japan for this dish, consisting of thinly sliced meat (usually beef), several vegetables and fresh mushrooms, to be prepared at the table. In fact, preparing the food is almost a ceremony, with each guest cooking his own food. Here are the ingredients the hostess for the dinner should have ready:

¾ lb. (400 g.) beef tenderloin or sirloin
¾ lb. (400 g.) veal fillet (loin)
6 to 8 cups (1½ to 2 liters) broth
Salt. Pepper. Soy sauce. Sugar
Sherry (or sake)
2 lbs. (1 kg.) vegetables (cauliflowerets, onion and green pepper rings, strips of leek and endive, slices of kohlrabi and bamboo shoots)
4 egg yolks. Tomato ketchup
Mayonnaise sauces, mixed pickles, and small onions

Cut meat into ⅛-inch (3-millimeter) slices and arrange on serving plates. Pour broth into fondue pot and season to taste with salt, pepper, soy sauce, sugar and sherry. Place on an alcohol burner at the table. Prepare and cut vegetables. Add part or all of the vegetables to the broth.
Serve each guest one lightly beaten egg yolk in a small bowl. Serve flavorful sauces and other side dishes separately (see sauces for Fondue Bourguignonne). Each guest spears a slice of meat with the fondue fork and dips it into the boiling vegetable broth. He then dips the cooked meat in the egg yolk or one of the sauces and eats it with a vegetable morsel from the pot or with one of the side dishes. Serve with fluffy hot rice.
4 servings

Note: In many modern restaurants sukiyaki is prepared in the following manner. Brown thinly sliced *sirloin of beef* in hot oil in an electric skillet; add a mixture of about *2 tablespoons* (20 grams or ½ ounce) sugar, *6 tablespoons* (90 milliliters) soy sauce, and 2 teaspoons water. Push beef to one side and add thinly sliced *onions, green pepper* and *celery.* Cook quickly, about 3 minutes. Add *bamboo shoots,* sliced fresh *mushrooms* and sliced *green onion* tops. Cook 2 or 3 minutes adding more soy sauce, if needed.

Tarator
Bulgaria

This cold soup is especially popular in the Near East and is made with yogurt, walnuts and a fresh vegetable such as cucumber or green pepper. Other countries have similar versions of Tarator; for example, Gazpacho from Spain, Dschadschik from Turkey and Okroschka from Russia. Yogurt, called "podkwassa" in Bulgaria, is considered a most nutritious food. In fact, the people from the Balkans are convinced of the wholesome and life-prolonging properties of soured milk.

Statistics state proudly that there are hundreds of persons in Bulgaria who are over 100 years old, and apparently one of them has celebrated his 119th birthday.

During the last decade, eating yogurt has become popular in many countries. If indeed the very old age of some Bulgarians is attributable to yogurt, then the number of 100-year-olds should soon increase rapidly all over the world.

1 large cucumber, pared and shredded. Salt
2 garlic cloves, crushed. 2 to 3 tablespoons oil
¾ cup (100 g. or 3½ oz.) walnuts
3 cups (¾ liter or about 1½ pt.) yogurt
½ cup (⅛ liter or about ¼ pt.) sour cream
Pepper. 2 tablespoons finely chopped dill

Shred or finely dice cucumber. Sprinkle with salt and refrigerate several hours. Combine garlic, oil, walnuts and yogurt in container of electric blender. Blend until creamy. Blend in sour cream and season to taste with pepper. Combine yogurt mixture and shredded cucumber; sprinkle top with fresh dill and additional coarsely chopped walnuts. Serve icy cold. If desired, put 2 or 3 ice cubes into each soup bowl.
About 6 servings

Tempura
Japan

The Japanese learned the preparation of this dish from the Portuguese, who by the sixteenth century had begun a brisk trading with the Japanese. The Portuguese did not eat meat on the four Ember Days (called by the Latin name Quattor Tempora). Instead they ate seafood. Thus the name Tempura was given to the fried shrimp that the Portuguese became fond of while in Japan. After the departure of the Portuguese, the Japanese continued to improve upon the Portuguese Tempura, using a more delicate batter for coating not only seafood, but also morsels of chicken, meat and vegetables. Tempura is often accompanied with a piquant dipping sauce.

8 oz. (250 g.) perch or sea salmon fillets
8 oz. (250 g.) shrimp; halved if large
2 large onions, sliced and separated
½ head cauliflower, separated in flowerets
1 eggplant, halved lengthwise, halves sliced ¼ in. thick
Salt. Pepper. Lemon juice
Fat for deep-frying, heated to 375°F (190°C)

Batter:
1 egg yolk. 2 cups (½ liter or about 1 pt.) cold water
2¼ cups (250 g. or 9 oz.) flour. ⅛ teaspoon baking soda
2 tablespoons (18 g.) cornstarch
¼ teaspoon monosodium glutamate

Sauce:
4 tablespoons sherry or sake. 4 tablespoons soy sauce
Salt. ½ cup (⅛ liter) beef or fish broth
1 small piece finely chopped ginger root
Icicle white radish, coarsely shredded

Cut fish fillets into bite-sized pieces. Season fish, shrimp and vegetables with salt and pepper. Sprinkle with lemon juice and set aside about 30 minutes.
Combine egg yolk with cold water. Mix flour and next 3 ingredients. Combine mixtures and beat until smooth. Dip fish and vegetables in batter and deep-fry in hot fat until golden.
Combine sherry, soy sauce, salt and broth. Heat and add ginger root. Cool; pour over radish or spinach in bowls.
4 to 6 servings

90

Tournedos
France

Tournedos are small fillet steaks cut from the thin end of the beef tenderloin. Each steak is usually about 1 inch (2½ centimeters) thick and 2½ inches (6½ centimeters) in diameter. Its name derives from the French verb tourner, meaning to turn and the French noun "dos" meaning "back" Tournedos are often prepared with strips of bacon or pork fat wrapped around the outside edge. The tournedos are then tied with string to help keep their round shape. After cooking, the string is removed. The Italian composer, Gioacchino Rossini (1792-1868), was the creator of the tournedos served with pâté de foie gras (goose liver) and truffles. It seems that Rossini was not only a successful and prolific composer of operas, but also a gourmet cook. It was said that he was much more interested in cooking than in composing music.

4 tournedos, cut 1½ in. (4 cm.) thick
4 narrow slices bacon. Fat for frying. Salt. Pepper
1 slice pâté de fois gras. 1 small piece of goose liver
1 truffle. 1 tomato. Asparagus spears
Dill. Parsley. Chicken livers. Onion rings

Beat tournedos very slightly with a meat hammer, then push together so that they are round in shape. Wrap outside edge with a bacon slice and secure with string.

Heat a small amount of fat in a heavy skillet and add tournedos. Sauté 3 to 4 minutes on each side; season with salt and pepper. (If desired, the tournedos may be placed under broiler heat and cooked to personal taste.) Transfer to a heated platter. Serve with crisp salad.

Suggested garnishes: 1 slice *goose liver*, pieces of *truffle* (Tournedos à la Rossini), broiled *tomato slices*, *asparagus spears* and fresh *dill*, *parsley*, *fried chicken livers* and fried *onion rings*.

4 servings

Waldorf Salad
United States

John Jacob Astor (1763-1848) left his village of Walldorf (near Heidelberg) as a young man, and immigrated to America, where he acquired enormous wealth by dealing in furs and speculating in real estate. One of his own constructions was the Waldorf-Astoria Hotel in New York, a huge "palace of hospitality" with 1300 rooms. This salad comes from the kitchens of the "old" Waldorf-Astoria. The salad usually consisted of thin strips of celery and apples with chopped walnuts, tossed together with dressing. However, nowadays one will find all sorts of other ingredients used in salads having that name, including raisins, grapes, orange segments, pineapple pieces and shredded carrot.

8 oz. (250 g.) celery or use cooked celery root (celeriac)
2 medium apples
½ cup (100 g. or 3½ oz.) walnuts
½ cup (100 g.) mayonnaise
2 tablespoons lemon juice. Salt
4 tablespoons heavy cream

Clean celery stalks and cut in strips. Pare apples (or do not pare, if skin is tender); remove core and cut apples into strips. Blanch walnut halves, then toast (see note) and reserve 4 or 5 for garnishing. Mix mayonnaise with lemon juice and salt. Blend in the cream. Toss dressing with other salad ingredients, mixing well. Turn into a salad bowl and garnish with the reserved walnut halves. Chill until ready to serve.
4 servings

Note: To toast walnuts (keep them crisp), drop halves into rapidly boiling *water;* cook 3 minutes and drain thoroughly. Spread evenly in a shallow pan and heat in a moderate oven (350°F or 180°C) 15 to 20 minutes, stirring often. The walnuts should be crisp and golden. If desired, brush nuts with melted butter and sprinkle lightly with salt.

Waterzooi
Belgium

Waterzooi, an old Flemish specialty, is not only a favorite dish of Belgium but also one that is known throughout Europe. It is prepared by cooking fish or chicken in a rich stock made with white wine, vegetables and herbs.

Belgians like to eat well and copiously. Peter Brueghel, the famous Flemish artist, portrayed this pleasure in eating in his paintings of well-laden tables and corpulent eaters. Charles de Coster described Belgian high living in his ''Uilenspiegel'', and Felix Timmermans immortalized it in ''Pallieter''.

Here is a recipe for Waterzooi that uses fish as the basic ingredient.

4½ lbs. (2 kg.) fresh water fish (eel, pike, carp
or perch), cut in pieces
7 oz. (200 g.) celery root or celeriac, cut in strips
Soup greens (see note with Bollito Misto)
½ bay leaf. 6 peppercorns. White wine
8 tablespoons (100 g. or 4 oz.) butter. 3 lemon slices
White bread slices, toasted

Put fish and celery root into a large casserole. Add soup greens and seasonings. Pour in enough wine and *water* to cover mixture (2 parts water to 1 part wine). Add butter; cover and cook gently until fish flakes easily. Add lemon slices when fish is almost done. Remove fish; strain broth and thicken with zwieback or rusk crumbs. Add seasonings, if needed. Pour sauce over toast slices and serve fish separately.
6 to 8 servings

Chicken Waterzooi:
Using *5 pounds (2¼ kilograms) chicken,* cut up, brown on all sides in *butter* in a saucepot or casserole. Add *8 stalks celery, soup greens,* and *seasonings* (see recipe above). Cover with water and bring to boiling. Cook gently until chicken is tender. Remove chicken from stock. Strain stock and bring to boiling; add *1 lemon, thinly sliced,* and *1 table-spoon chopped parsley.* Stir in *3 egg yolks* beaten with several tablespoons *cream.* Heat and stir (do not boil). When sauce thickens slightly, return chicken and serve with *cracked wheat bread, toasted.*

Welsh Rabbit
England, United States

This dish, consisting of melted Cheddar cheese and ale or beer, has many variations. Welsh Rabbit is sometimes called Welsh Rarebit, the name often given in old cookbooks. Welsh Rabbit is served in various ways, but traditionally the melted cheese mixture is simply turned into a serving dish and each person dips cubes of bread into it. Today's hostess is likely to prepare Welsh Rabbit in a chafing dish at the table. Busy homemakers, especially, will appreciate the following modern quick and easy way to prepare Welsh Rabbit.

3 tablespoons milk
1 8-oz. jar (225 g.) pasteurized process cheese spread
1 teaspoon sharp prepared mustard. 1 dash pepper
½ teaspoon Worcestershire sauce
½ cup (⅛ liter or about ¼ pt.) light beer
12 slices white bread

Heat milk in a saucepan. Mix in the cheese spread and stir until thoroughly blended. Season with mustard, pepper and Worcestershire sauce. Add beer gradually, stirring until well blended. Heat mixture to serving temperature. Place slices of buttered toast on a plate or in a bowl and cover with the cheese mixture.
4 to 6 servings

Note: If desired, prepare Buck Rabbit by topping Welsh Rabbit with a freshly poached egg; or serve Welsh Rabbit with cooked bacon and sliced tomato.

Variation: Combine in top of a double boiler over simmering water 8 oz. *(2 cups, shredded) natural Cheddar cheese, ½ cup ale or beer, 2 tablespoons (25 g. or 1 oz.) butter or margarine, ½ teaspoon paprika,* and *⅛ teaspoon dry mustard.* Heat, stirring occasionally, until sauce is smooth. Blend in *1 egg, slightly beaten* and stir until thickened. Serve on toast.

Viennese Apple Strudel
Austria

Apple Strudel is one of the showpieces of Austrian desserts. Strudels are sometimes made using a yeast dough or puff pastry, but a traditional strudel consists of a simple dough that is stretched out so thinly that one can "read a love letter through it". The dough is spread with fruit, cheese, nuts, or other fillings, then rolled and baked. Apple Strudel is probably the most popular kind of strudel.

2¼ cups (250 g. or 9 oz.) flour. ½ teaspoon salt
3 tablespoons oil
¾ cup (175 ml. or about ⅓ pt.) lukewarm water
3½ lbs. (1½ kg.) tart apples
¾ cup (85 g. or 3 oz.) fine dry bread crumbs
⅔ cup (125 g. or 4½ oz.) sugar
1 tablespoon vanilla-flavored sugar
1 to 1½ teaspoons cinnamon
½ cup (75 g. or 2½ oz.) raisins
½ cup (75 g. or 2½ oz.) chopped almonds
½ to ¾ cup (100 to 150 g. or 4 to 6 oz.)
butter or margarine, melted

Put flour combined with salt onto a board. Make a well in the center; add oil and just enough water to make a dough that can be kneaded until smooth and elastic. Knead dough, using as little flour on board as possible. Form into a ball and let rest 20 to 30 minutes.

Pare, core and thinly slice apples. Combine apples, bread crumbs and a mixture of sugar, vanilla sugar and cinnamon. Add raisins and almonds. Toss to mix well.

Divide dough into 4 equal portions. Roll each portion on the floured board and as dough becomes thinner transfer it to a lightly floured cloth. Continue rolling and stretching until the dough is very thin. Lightly brush surface of dough with melted butter; spoon a fourth of the filling on each portion. Drizzle with melted butter. Roll up the dough and place on a greased baking sheet. Brush tops with some of the remaining melted butter so that the baked strudel will have a light golden crust. Bake in a hot oven (400°F or 200°C) 50 to 60 minutes. Before serving, sprinkle with *confectioners' sugar*.
4 small strudel rolls

Fried Chicken Viennese Style
Austria

According to Viennese tradition, this deep-fried chicken is accompanied with parsley sprigs also crisply fried in deep fat.

2 chickens (about 1½ lbs. or 700 g. each)
Salt. Pepper. Flour
2 eggs, slightly beaten
Fine dry bread crumbs
Lard for deep-frying, heated to 350°F (175°C)
1 bunch parsley

Prepare chicken and quarter. Rub the pieces with salt and pepper, coat with flour, dip in beaten eggs and then in bread crumbs. Heat fat (about 2 inches or 5 centimeters) deep in heavy skillet. Add chicken pieces and fry about 25 minutes, turning pieces to brown evenly. Transfer to shallow baking pan and pour melted *butter* or *margarine* over pieces. Place in moderate oven (350°F or 180°C) about 15 minutes, or until chicken is tender. Meanwhile, quickly fry the parsley in fat (increasing temperature to 390°F or 200°C). Arrange chicken on platter; garnish with *parsley* and *lemon wedges*. 4 to 6 servings

96

Wiener Schnitzel
Austria

Wiener Schnitzel is served all over the world as a representative of European cuisine. The word schnitzel is German for cutlet of meat, usually of veal. Wiener Schnitzel is simply a thin slice of veal, breaded and fried and sometimes topped with anchovies or capers.

4 veal cutlets. Salt. Flour. 1 egg, lightly beaten

Fine dry bread crumbs. Lemon slices. Anchovy fillets

Fat for frying, heated to 365-375°F (185 to 190°C)
Pound meat on one side with meat hammer. Turn and repeat process until cutlets are ¼ inch (1½ centimeters) thick. Sprinkle with salt, then coat with flour. Dip cutlets in egg and coat with bread crumbs. Heat a generous amount of fat in a deep heavy skillet; brown cutlets in the fat for 3 to 4 minutes on each side or until golden. Arrange on a platter and garnish each cutlet with a slice of lemon and rolled anchovy fillet. Serve with a tossed green salad. *4 servings*

97

Zabaione
Italy

Zabaione is a creamy dessert originating in Italy. It is made with egg yolks, sugar and wine, which are beaten to a light foam consistency. The wine used is Marsala, produced from grapes grown near the small town of Marsala in Sicily. Zabaione, sometimes formerly spelled Zabaglione, seems to have been known in Italy for many centuries. Tradition has it that the art of cooking Zabaione was the special knowledge of the cooks who accompanied the fourteen-year-old Catherine de Medici to France where, in 1533, she married Henry of Orleans, heir to the French throne. Frenchmen learned from her cooks how to prepare not only Sabayon (as Zabaione is called in France), but also many other Italian gourmet specialties that are now included in French cuisine. In France, Sabayon is generally served as a sauce over cake, ice cream, or fresh fruit instead of being served as a dessert to be eaten with a spoon.

6 egg yolks. ¼ cup (50 g. or 2 oz.) sugar
1 teaspoon vanilla-flavored sugar
½ cup (⅛ liter or about ¼ pt.) Marsala
1 dash maraschino

Using a rotary beater, beat the egg yolks with the sugar and vanilla sugar until very thick. Blend in the Marsala and mara-schino, beating constantly. Turn mixture into top of a double bciler and cook over simmering water; continue beating until mixture is very light and begins to rise to top of double boiler. Immediately remove from heat. Serve warm or cold in large glasses.
About 6 servings

Note: For French Sabayon, increase wine to 1 cup (¼ liter or about ½ pint). For a warm sauce to serve over cake or ice cream, use *sweet white wine;* for a cold sauce over fresh fruit, use either sweet wine or a *dry white wine.*

98

Zuger Kirschtorte
Switzerland

This famous Swiss torte is named for the Swiss town of Zug which produces the cherries from which kirsch is made. The center layer of this delightful cake is saturated with a syrup made with kirsch, and the kirsch flavor permeates the torte.

7 egg whites
3 cups (360 g. or 12 oz.) confectioners' sugar
8 tablespoons (24 g. or 1 oz.) cornstarch
3½ oz. (100 g.) filberts, finely grated. 4 egg yolks
3 tablespoons hot water. ½ cup (50 g. or 2 oz.) flour
¼ teaspoon baking powder. 4 tablespoons water
½ cup (⅛ liter or about ¼ pt.) kirsch
¾ cup (170 g. or 6 oz.) butter. 3 tablespoons red jelly
4½ oz. (125 g.) chopped roasted filberts

For Nut Torte Layers:
Beat 4 egg whites until peaks are formed. Gradually add 1 cup sugar, 7 teaspoons cornstarch and grated nuts, beating until blended. Divide equally in two aluminum foil-lined 9-inch layer cake pans. Bake in a slow oven (325°F or 160°C) 20 to 25 minutes. Cool slightly and peel off foil.

For Cake Layer:
Beat 3 egg yolks with hot water until fluffy. Beat in ⅔ cup sugar until blended. Beat 3 egg whites with 1½ tablespoons sugar until peaks are formed. Fold egg yolks into egg whites. Sift flour, remaining cornstarch and baking powder over the top. Mix until blended. Turn into an aluminum foil-lined 9-inch layer cake pan. Bake in a moderate oven (350°F or 180°C) 20 to 25 minutes. Cool slightly and peel off foil.

For Kirsch Syrup:
Bring water with 3 tablespoons sugar to boiling. Let cool and add kirsch.

For Butter Cream:
Cream butter with 1¼ cups sugar until fluffy. Beat in remaining egg yolk and jelly.

Spread first torte layer with butter cream. Pour syrup over cake layer and place on top of the first torte layer. Spread again with butter cream and top with the second torte layer. Cover entire torte with butter cream, sprinkle sides with nuts and cover surface with remaining sugar.
10 to 12 servings

Zuppa Pavese
Italy

This unique soup is a specialty of Pavia. The legend about this dish resembles the German story of the Kaiserschmarrn. In 1525, King Francis I of France, fleeing defeat at the hands of Emperor Charles V of Spain, was driven by hunger to stop at a small farmhouse near Pavia. The farmer's wife had nothing in the house except a little broth, a few slices of bread, some cheese and several eggs. Quickly, she toasted the bread, poured broth over it, and added an egg and some cheese and the royal soup was ready. Francis I of France has long ago been forgotten; not so the Zuppa Pavese, which is known everywhere.

4 cups (1 liter or about 2 pts.) chicken broth
4 slices (½ inch or 13 millimeters thick) bread,
toasted and generously buttered
4 eggs. 4 tablespoons freshly grated Parmesan cheese

Heat the chicken broth, adding more seasoning, if needed. Prepare buttered toast and place slices in individual soup bowls. Break an egg over each bread slice. Carefully pour broth into bowls, taking care not to break the egg yolks.
Place in a moderate oven (350°F or 180°C) and bake until the egg white is firm. Before serving, sprinkle generously with grated cheese.
4 servings

Note: Instead of toasting and buttering the bread, the slices may be browned on both sides in butter in a skillet or on a griddle. If desired, use poached eggs and omit oven cooking.

To poach eggs, grease the bottom of a small skillet. Add *water* to a 2-inch (5-centimeter) depth or enough to come 1 inch above the eggs. Lightly *salt* the water; bring to boiling, then reduce heat to simmering. Break the eggs, one at a time, into a small dish and slip each into the water. Cook 3 to 5 minutes depending on firmness desired. Remove with slotted spoon.

100

Weights

Ounces	Grams	Kilogram(s)
1	25	
2	50	
2½	75	
3	85	
3½	100	
4	115	⅛
4½	125	
5	150	
6	170	
7	200	
8	225	¼
9	250	
10	275	
11	300	
12	350	
13	375	
14	400	
15	425	

Pounds		
1	450-500	½
1½	700	
1¾	750	
2		1
3½		1½
4½		2

Liquid Measures

Australia (Avoirdupois)	Metric	British Imperial
½ cup	⅛ liter	about ¼ pint
¾ cup	2 deciliters	about ⅓ pint
1 cup	¼ liter (2½ deciliters)	about ½ pint
1½ cups	⅜ liter	about ¾ pint
2 cups	½ liter (1 demiliter)	about 1 pint
2½ cups	⅝ liter	about 1¼ pints
3 cups	¾ liter (7½ deciliters)	about 1½ pints
4 cups	1 liter	about 2 pints

Linear Measures

Inch(es)	Centimeter(s)
¼	½
⅜	1
½	1¼
1	2½
1½	4
2	5
2½	6½
3	8
3½	9
4	10
5	13
6	15
7	18
8	20
9	23

Temperatures

Fahrenheit	Centigrade	Oven Heat
300°	150°	slow
325°	160°	slow
350°	180°	moderate
375°	190°	moderately hot
400°	200°	hot
425°	220°	hot
450°	230°	very hot
475°	245°	very hot
500°	260°	extremely hot

The countries

Germany
Green Sauce	37
Lucca-Äugen (Lucca-Eyes)	52
Pichelsteiner (Stew)	64
Sauerbraten (Rhineland Style)	72
Schnitzel Holstein	82
Soufflé Fürst Pückler	87

Hungary
Beef à la Esterházy	30
Gulyáshus	38

India
Chicken Curry	41
Kedgeree	50
Mulligatawny Soup	55

Indonesia
Nasi Goreng	57

Ireland
Irish Stew	46

Israel
Gefillte Fish (Stuffed Whole Fish)	34

Italy
Bollito Misto	6
Cannelloni	12
Green Sauce	37
Minestrone	53
Ossobucco	59
Pasta Asciutta	62
Pizza	65
Risotto	73
Saltimbocca	75
Zabaione	98
Zuppa Pavese	100

Japan
Sukiyaki	88
Tempura	90

Mexico
Chili con Carne	20
Enchiladas	28

Netherlands
Hutspot	44

North Africa
Kuskus	51

Orient
Musaka	56
Shaslik (Shish Kebab)	80

Poland
Bigos	3
Polish Carp	49

South America
Olla Podrida	58

Soviet Union
Beef Stroganoff	5
Borscht	7
Charlotte Russe	16
Shaslik (Shish Kebab)	80
Solianka	86
Strawberries Romanoff	29

Spain
Olla Podrida	58
Paella	60

Switzerland
Bern Councillors' Plate	2
Fondue Bourguignonne	31
Fondue Neuchâteloise	32
Trout with Almonds	33
Veal Scallops	36
Veal Steak Cordon Bleu	48
Zuger Kirschtorte	99

Turkey
Dolmas	26
Imam Bayildi	45
Mutton Pilaf	39

United States
Boston Baked Beans	8
Cheesecake	18
Chicken Salad with Celery	35
Chop Suey	21
Clam Chowder	22
Lobster Cocktail	43
Waldorf Salad	92
Welsh Rabbit	94

Yugoslavia
Cevapcíci	15
Culbastija	24
Duvede	25
Sarma	77
Sataras	78

The recipes in groups

Schnitzel Holstein (Germany)	82	
Shaslik (Shish Kebab) (Soviet Union, Orient)	80	
Sukiyaki (Japan)	88	
Sweet and Sour Pork (China)	83	
Tournedos (France)	91	
Veal Scallops (Switzerland)	36	
Veal Steak Cordon Bleu (Switzerland)	48	
Wiener Schnitzel (Austria)	97	

Pasta and Rice

Cannelloni (Italy)	12
Kedgeree (India)	50
Mutton Pilaf (Turkey)	39
Nasi Goreng (Indonesia)	57
Paella (Spain)	60
Pasta Ascuitta (Italy)	62
Risotto (Italy)	73

Poultry

Canard à l'Orange (France)	11
Chicken Curry (India)	41
Chicken Marengo (France)	40
Fried Chicken Viennese Style (Austria)	96
Poularde de Bruxelles (Belgium)	10

Salads

Chicken Salad with Celery (United States)	35
Chicory Salad (Belgium)	19
Waldorf Salad (United States)	92

Sauce

Green Sauce (Italy and Germany)	37

Sandwich

Smorrebrod (Denmark)	85

Soups

Borscht (Soviet Union)	7
Clam Chowder (United States)	22
Minestrone (Italy)	53
Mock Turtle Soup (England)	54
Mulligatawny Soup (India and England)	55
Solianka (Soviet Union)	86
Tarator (Bulgaria)	89
Turtle Soup (England)	81
Zuppa Pavese (Italy)	100

Stews and Other Main Dishes

Bigos (Poland)	3
Carbonada Criolla (Argentina)	13
Cassoulet (France)	14
Chop Suey (United States and China)	21
Enchiladas (Mexico)	28
Gulyáshus (Hungary)	38
Hutspot (Netherlands)	44
Irish Stew (Ireland)	46
Kuskus (North Africa)	51
Musaka (Orient)	56
Olla Podrida (Spain, South America)	58

Pichelsteiner (Stew) (Germany)	64
Ragoût Fin (France)	68
Sataras (Yugoslavia)	78

Vegetables

Boston Baked Beans (United States, Canada)	8
Dolmas (Turkey)	26
Imam Bayildi (Turkey)	45
Ratatouille (France)	69
Sarma (Yugoslavia)	77